MW01008678

EDITOR: Maryanne Blacker

FOOD EDITOR: Pamela Clark

DESIGN DIRECTOR: Neil Carlyle

• • •

TEST KITCHEN STAFF:

ASSISTANT FOOD EDITORS:
Jan Castorina, Karen Green

ASSOCIATE FOOD EDITOR: Enid Morrison

CHIEF HOME ECONOMIST: Kathy Wharton

HOME ECONOMISTS: Tracey Kern, Quinton Kohler,
Jill Lange, Alexandra McCowan, Kathy McGarry,
Louise Patniotis, Dimitra Stais

EDITORIAL ASSISTANT: Elizabeth Gray

KITCHEN ASSISTANT: Amy Wong

• • •

HOME LIBRARY STAFF:

ASSISTANT EDITOR: Judy Newman

SUB-EDITOR: Danielle Farah

ART DIRECTOR: Robbylee Phelan

CADET ARTIST: Louise McGeachie

SECRETARY: Wendy Moore

• • •

PUBLISHER: Richard Walsh

DEPUTY PUBLISHER: Graham Lawrence

• • •

Produced by The Australian Women's Weekly
Home Library
Typeset by Photoset Computer Service Pty Ltd,
and Letter Perfect, Sydney.
Printed by Dai Nippon Co Ltd, Tokyo, Japan
Published by Australian Consolidated Press,
54 Park Street Sydney
Distributed by Network Distribution Company,
54 Park Street Sydney
Distributed in the U.K. by Australian Consolidated Press (UK)
Ltd (0604) 760 456. Distributed in Canada
by Whitecap Books Ltd (604) 980 9852. Distributed in South
Africa by Intermag (011) 493 3200.

• • •

Best Ever Recipes.

Includes index.
ISBN 0 949128 27 9.

1. Cookery. (Series: Australian Women's
Weekly Home Library)

641.5

• • •

FRONT COVER: Turkey, page 41.
China from The Country Trader; carving knife and fork from
Appley Hoare Antiques; table and chair from Country Form
BACK COVER: Snow-White Cheesecake, page 76.
China from Mikasa; table from Country Form
OPPOSITE: Orange Brandy Cream Biscuits, page 86.

From the famous cookery pages of The Australian Women's
Weekly come former Food Editor Pamela Clark's favourite
recipes to star at your table. They're mostly for family meals
(including tasty, economical sausages, rice and pasta, and
vegetarian dishes). For special occasions, you can easily make
up a menu for a formal dinner, a buffet or afternoon tea from
the tempting ideas throughout the book.

Pamela Clark
FOOD EDITOR

BRITISH & NORTH AMERICAN READERS: Please note that conversion charts for cup
and spoon measurements and oven temperatures are on page 128.

Glossary

Here are some terms, names and alternatives to help everyone use and understand our recipes perfectly.

ALCOHOL: is optional but gives special flavour; you can use fruit juice or water instead to make up the liquid content.

ALLSPICE, WHOLE: pimento.

ALMONDS, GROUND: we used packaged, commercially ground nuts in our recipes unless otherwise specified.

APPLES, COOKING: we used Granny Smith apples.

BACON RASHERS: bacon slices.

BAKING POWDER: a raising agent consisting of an alkali and an acid. It is mostly made from cream of tartar and bicarbonate of soda in the proportions of 1 level teaspoon of cream of tartar to ½ level teaspoon bicarbonate of soda. This is equivalent to 2 teaspoons baking powder.

BEAN CURD: also known as tofu.

BEEF:

Chuck Steak: is cut from the neck of the animal.

Minced Beef: ground beef.

Topside Steak: is cut from the hind leg.

BICARBONATE OF SODA: baking soda.

BREADCRUMBS:

Fresh: use 1 or 2 day old white bread made into crumbs by grating, blending or processing.

Packaged: use fine packaged breadcrumbs.

BUTTER: use salted or unsalted (sweet) butter; 125g is equal to 1 stick butter.

CHESTNUT:

Puree: an unsweetened puree of chestnuts. Do not confuse with the sweetened flavoured chestnut spread.

Spread: sweetened, flavoured pureed chestnuts.

CHICKEN: we used several different types of chicken in this book. Size is determined by numbering system; for example, No 13 is a 1.3kg bird; No 10 is 1kg. This system applies to most poultry.

CHOCOLATE:

Dark: we used good-quality cooking chocolate.

Drinking: sweetened powdered chocolate.

CINNAMON: fragrant bark used as a spice in ground form or sticks (quills).

COCONUT: use desiccated unless otherwise specified.

COINTREAU: orange-flavoured liqueur.

COPHA: a solid white shortening based on coconut oil. Kremelta and Palmin can be substituted.

CORNFLOUR: cornstarch.

CREAM, SOUR: a thick commercially-cultured sour cream.

CREME DE CACAO: chocolate-flavoured liqueur.

CREME DE MENTHE: mint-flavoured liqueur.

CUSTARD POWDER: pudding mix.

EGGPLANT: aubergine.

ESSENCE: an extract from fruit and flowers, used as a flavouring.

FIVE SPICE POWDER: a pungent mixture of ground spices which include cinnamon, cloves, fennel, star anise and Szechwan peppers.

FLOUR:

White Plain: all-purpose flour.

White Self-Raising: substitute plain (all-purpose) flour and baking powder in the proportion of ¾ metric cup plain flour to 2 level metric teaspoons of baking powder. Sift together several times before using. If using 8oz measuring cup, use 1 metric cup plain flour to 2 level metric teaspoons baking powder.

Wholemeal Plain: wholewheat flour without the addition of baking powder.

Wholemeal Self-Raising: wholewheat self-raising flour; add baking powder as above to make wholemeal self-raising flour.

GINGER:

Fresh, Green or Root Ginger: scrape away outside skin and grate, chop or slice ginger as required.

Ground: is not a substitute for fresh ginger.

Preserved: ginger which has been cooked and stored in a thick sugar syrup. Available from most supermarkets.

GOLDEN SYRUP: maple, pancake syrup or honey can be substituted.

GRAND MARNIER: orange-flavoured liqueur.

HAZELNUTS, GROUND: use packaged ground nuts unless otherwise specified.

HERBS: we have specified when to use fresh or dried herbs. We used dried (not ground) herbs in the proportion of 1:4 for fresh herbs; eg, 1 teaspoon dried herbs instead of 4 teaspoons (1 tablespoon) chopped fresh herbs.

JAM: conserve.

KIWI FRUIT: also known as Chinese gooseberry.

LIQUID GLUCOSE (glucose syrup): made from wheat starch; available at health food stores and supermarkets.

MILK: We used full-cream homogenised milk unless otherwise specified.

Evaporated: milk condensed by evaporation, sterilised by heat and canned.

Sweetened condensed: we used Nestle's milk which has had 60 percent of the water removed, then sweetened with sugar.

MIXED FRUIT: a combination of sultanas, raisins, currants, mixed peel and cherries.

MIXED PEEL: a mixture of crystallised citrus peel; also known as candied peel.

MIXED SPICE: a finely ground combination of spices which includes allspice, nutmeg and cinnamon; used as an ingredient in sweet recipes.

MUSHROOMS, STRAW: available in cans, champignons can be subsituted.

MUSTARD SEEDS: tiny seeds used in curries, pickling and making mustard; seeds can be black (spicy and piquant), brown (less

piquant) or white (yellow in colour and milder in flavour).

PAPAW: large yellow tropical fruit, known in some countries as papaya.

PEPPERS: capsicum or bell peppers.

PORK SPARERIBS: pork rashers, cut from the belly of pork.

PRAWNS: shrimp.

PUNNET: small containers usually for berries. May be 200g or 250g.

RICE, GROUND: rice flour can be substituted.

RIND: zest.

RUM: we used underproof dark rum.

SESAME:

Oil: made from roasted, crushed white sesame seeds, is an aromatic golden-coloured oil with a nutty flavour. It is always used in small quantities and added mostly towards the end of the cooking time. It is not the same as the sesame oil sold in health food stores and should not be used to fry food. It is a flavouring only and can be bought in supermarkets and Asian food stores.

Seeds: there are 2 types of sesame seeds, black and white; we used the white variety in this book.

SOUR CREAM: a thick commercially cultured soured cream.

SOY SAUCE: made from fermented soy beans. The light sauce is generally used with white meat for flavour, and the darker variety with red meat for colour. There is a multi-purpose salt-reduced sauce available, also Japanese soy sauce. It is personal taste which sauce you use.

SUGAR: We used coarse granulated table sugar, also known as crystal sugar, unless otherwise specified.

Brown: a soft fine-granulated sugar with molasses present which gives it its characteristic colour.

Castor: fine granulated table sugar.

Icing: also known as confectioners' sugar or powdered sugar. We used icing sugar mixture, not pure icing sugar, unless specified.

TAHINI PASTE: made from crushed sesame seeds.

TARAMA: smoked cod's roe. Available in cans or fresh from most delicatessens.

TIA MARIA: coffee-flavoured liqueur.

TOMATO SAUCE: tomato ketchup.

VANILLA: we used imitation extract.

VEGETABLE JUICE: we used V8 vegetable juice which is a mixture of tomato, carrot, celery, beetroot, parsley, lettuce, watercress and spinach. It is available in cans and cartons from most supermarkets.

YEAST: allow 3 teaspoons (7g) dried granulated yeast to each 15g compressed yeast.

ZUCCHINI: courgette.

Soups

Here are hearty soups full of flavour; some a meal in themselves

CURRIED PEA SOUP
500g (1lb) pkt frozen peas
60g (2oz) butter
3 tablespoons flour
2 teaspoons curry powder
4 cups water
3 chicken stock cubes
½ cup cream or milk
2 tablespoons chopped mint
salt, pepper

Drop peas into boiling salted water, reduce heat, cook until tender; approximately 7 minutes. Drain, push peas through sieve or blend in blender. Heat butter in pan, add flour and curry powder, stir until combined, remove pan from heat. Gradually add water, stir until combined. Return pan to heat, add crumbled stock cubes, stir until soup boils and thickens. Reduce heat, add pureed peas, cream or milk and mint; mix well. Simmer, uncovered, 5 minutes. Season with salt and pepper. Serves 4 to 6.

GOULASH SOUP
30g (1oz) butter
2 large onions
2 large carrots
3 sticks celery
500g (1lb) pork (see Note)
125g (4oz) bacon pieces
2 tablespoons paprika
60g (2oz) butter, extra
2 tablespoons oil
½ cup flour
2 litres (8 cups) water
2 beef stock cubes
2 chicken stock cubes
¼ teaspoon caraway seeds

salt, pepper
⅓ cup tomato paste
3 tablespoons chopped parsley
cream

Heat butter in large pan, add peeled and chopped onions and carrots and chopped celery. Saute gently until golden brown, remove from pan. Add extra butter and oil to pan, add pork and bacon pieces. Cook gently until meat is golden brown, remove from pan. Add flour to pan, stir until dark golden brown. Add paprika, stir 1 minute more. Remove pan from heat, add water, stir until combined. Return pan to heat, stir until soup comes to boil, reduce heat. Add pork, bacon and vegetables, stir until combined. Add

Curried pea soup.

3

caraway seeds, beef and chicken stock cubes and tomato paste. Stir until combined, season with salt and pepper. Cover, simmer gently 1½ hours. Remove meat from soup. Push soup through sieve. Return soup to pan. Cut meat into small pieces, add to soup. Add parsley, heat until boiling. Spoon into serving dishes, swirl a little cream on top of each. Serves 6 to 8.

Note: Two large thick pork chops can be used for this soup; or ask your butcher for any economical cut of lean pork.

IRISH CHOWDER
750g (1½lb) gravy beef
⅓ cup dry lima beans
¼ cup split peas
¼ cup barley
2 litres (8 cups) water
2 carrots
2 onions
2 sticks celery
6 medium potatoes
1 pkt chicken noodle soup
salt, pepper
chopped parsley

Remove any excess fat from meat, cut meat into cubes. Put meat, lima beans, split peas, barley, salt and water in large saucepan. Cover, bring to boil, reduce heat, simmer 45 minutes. Add sliced carrots, onions, celery, whole peeled potatoes and dry soup powder. Season with salt and pepper. Simmer, covered, 1 hour or until lima beans are tender. Stir in chopped parsley. A little extra water may be needed if mixture appears too thick. Serves 6.

EASY SPINACH SOUP
60g (2oz) butter
1 large onion
1 large potato
2 tablespoons chopped parsley
315g (10oz) pkt spinach-in-butter-sauce
3 cups water
4 chicken stock cubes
salt, pepper
2.5cm (1in) strip lemon rind

Put butter, peeled and chopped onion and potato and remaining ingredients into pan, bring to boil. Reduce heat, simmer covered 20 minutes or until potato is tender: remove lemon rind. Put soup into

blender, blend on medium speed until smooth. Return soup to pan, bring to boil, remove from heat. A little cream or sour cream can be swirled on top of each serving. Serves 4.

FRENCH ONION SOUP
4 large onions
60g (2oz) butter
1 teaspoon sugar
2 teaspoons flour
2 x 470g (15oz) cans beef consomme
3 cups water
pepper
8 slices white bread
250g (8oz) cheddar or gruyere cheese
60g (2oz) grated parmesan cheese

Heat butter in large saucepan, add peeled and sliced onions, saute until onions are tender and golden brown. Add sugar and flour, stir until combined, stir in consomme and water, bring to boil; reduce heat, simmer, covered, 30 minutes. Season with pepper. (Canned soup usually contains enough salt). Cut bread slices into 10cm (4in) rounds, toast slices. Grate cheddar cheese, combine with parmesan, cover bread rounds with cheese, put under griller until cheese is golden brown. Put one cheese slice into each bowl, pour hot soup over. Serves 8.

BEAN AND VEGETABLE SOUP
30g (1oz) butter
500g (1lb) gravy beef
3 litres (12 cups) water
1 teaspoon salt
125g (4oz) haricot beans
60g (2oz) butter, extra
2 large onions
125g (4oz) bacon pieces
2 large carrots
2 sticks celery
2 potatoes
500g (1lb) peas
3 tomatoes
1 cup shredded cabbage
salt, pepper

Cut meat into large pieces. Heat butter in large pan, add meat, brown well on all sides. Add water and salt, bring to boil. Reduce heat, simmer, covered, 1 hour. Add beans, simmer, covered, further 1 hour. Strain stock into large bowl, discard meat and return beans to stock. Heat extra butter in pan,

add peeled and chopped onions and chopped bacon pieces. Saute gently until onions are golden brown. Add peeled and diced carrots, sliced celery, peeled and diced potatoes, shelled peas and chopped tomatoes, cook further 2 minutes. Add vegetables to stock, stir until combined. Season with salt and pepper. Bring to boil, reduce heat, simmer, covered, 30 minutes. In last 5 minutes of cooking time add cabbage. Serves 6 to 8.

CREAM OF SPINACH SOUP
315g (10oz) pkt chopped frozen spinach
2 chicken stock cubes
2 tablespoons flour
salt, pepper
2 cups water
1 small onion
pinch nutmeg
1 rasher bacon
30g (1oz) butter
1 cup cream

Allow frozen spinach to thaw. Heat butter in saucepan, saute finely chopped bacon until tender. Put spinach, crumbled stock cubes, flour, salt, pepper, water, peeled and roughly chopped onion and nutmeg in blender. Blend on high speed until smooth. Pour into saucepan with bacon, stir over heat until soup boils. Reduce heat, simmer 5 minutes. Stir in cream, reheat gently. Serves 4.

PUMPKIN VICHYSSOISE
750g (1½lb) pumpkin
2 leeks or 2 large onions
250g (8oz) potatoes
3 chicken stock cubes
1 litre (4 cups) water
1 cup cream
salt, pepper

Peel pumpkin, cut into small pieces, put into large saucepan. Add sliced leeks or peeled and chopped onions, peeled and chopped potatoes, crumbled stock cubes and water. Bring to boil, reduce heat; simmer, uncovered, 25 minutes or until vegetables are very soft and tender; push vegetables and liquid through fine sieve or puree in blender. Return puree to saucepan, add cream, salt and pepper. Bring to boil, stirring; reduce heat, simmer further 5 minutes. Serves 6.

Goulash soup.

Pates & Dips

They're wonderful for parties, with drinks, or while the steaks are cooking on the barbecue

VEAL AND HAM TERRINE

500g (1lb) ham fat
500g (1lb) chicken livers
90g (3oz) butter
1 large onion
125g (4oz) mushrooms
4 rashers bacon
500g (1lb) minced veal
125g (4oz) minced pork
250g (8oz) ham pieces
3 eggs
½ cup cream
salt, pepper
2 tablespoons brandy
3 tablespoons port
¼ teaspoon thyme
2 bayleaves

Ask delicatessen for good-sized pieces of ham fat, about 15cm (6in) square, if you can get them. Slice ham fat thinly. Line base and sides of ovenproof dish (approximately 5-cup capacity) with fat. There should be enough fat left over to cover top of terrine when it is completed. Put chicken livers into cold salted water, allow to stand 30 minutes, drain, rinse well. Remove any tissue from livers, then chop livers very finely. Heat butter in frying pan, add peeled and very finely chopped onion, very finely chopped mushrooms and very finely chopped bacon. Saute gently until onion is tender. Put onion mixture, chicken livers, veal, pork, very finely chopped ham, beaten eggs, cream, salt, pepper, brandy, port and thyme into

Veal and ham terrine.

Pâtés & Dips

bowl, mix very well. Pour mixture into prepared dish, spreading out evenly. Cover meat completely with thin slices of remaining fat. Arrange bayleaves decoratively on top. Cover dish completely with aluminium foil. Put into baking dish with enough water to come half-way up sides of dish. Bake in moderate oven 2 hours. Cool, refrigerate overnight. Serves 8.

CRAB AND SALMON PATE

60g (2oz) butter
2 tablespoons plain flour
½ cup milk
½ cup cream
⅓ cup dry white wine
salt, pepper
1 teaspoon french mustard
250g (8oz) can red salmon
220g (7oz) can crab
3 teaspoons gelatine
¼ cup water

Heat butter in pan, add flour, stir until combined, remove pan from heat. Add milk and cream, stir until combined. Return pan to heat, stir until sauce boils and thickens. Reduce heat, simmer 2 minutes, remove pan from heat. Gradually stir in wine. Season with salt and pepper. Add mustard, mix well. Combine gelatine and water, add to white sauce mixture. Return pan to heat, stir for 4 minutes; do not boil. Put sauce into electric blender, add undrained salmon with bones and any dark skin removed. Blend on medium speed 2 minutes or until very smooth. Add undrained flaked crab, mix well (do not blend). Pour into 4 individual bowls. Cover bowls, refrigerate several hours or overnight. Serve with melba toast. Serves 4.

FISH PATE

125g (4oz) butter
500g (1lb) fish fillets
½ cup dry white wine
salt, pepper
½ cup cream
1 chicken stock cube

½ cup mayonnaise
1 teaspoon grated lemon rind

Remove skin and all bones from fish, cut fish into large pieces. Melt butter in pan, add fish, wine, salt, pepper and crumbled stock cube. Cover, bring to boil, reduce heat, simmer 5 minutes or until fish is just cooked. Remove fish from liquid. Bring liquid to boil, boil uncovered until about ¼ cup liquid remains. Add cream, stir until combined. Put fish in blender, add cream mixture. Blend on medium speed until smooth. Spoon into serving dish or individual dishes, refrigerate until firm. Combine mayonnaise and lemon rind, and spoon mixture over pate. Refrigerate. Serves 4.

CHICKEN LIVER PATE

¾ cup hot water
2 chicken stock cubes
1½ teaspoons gelatine
2 tablespoons cold water
parsley
1kg (2lb) chicken livers
⅓ cup brandy
90g (3oz) butter
6 rashers bacon
2 large onions
½ teaspoon thyme
1 bayleaf
⅓ cup dry sherry
⅔ cup cream
salt, pepper
150g (5oz) butter, extra

Put hot water and crumbled stock cubes into saucepan. Sprinkle gelatine over cold water, add to saucepan, stir until combined. Bring to boil, remove from heat, allow to cool. Pour enough chicken stock into oiled 23cm by 12cm (9in by 5in) loaf tin to just cover bottom. Refrigerate until set; refrigerate remaining stock until partially set. Arrange parsley sprigs decoratively over set layer, carefully spoon over remaining partially-set stock, refrigerate until firm. Chop chicken livers roughly, place in bowl, pour over brandy, marinate 1½ hours. Drain livers. Heat 45g (1½oz) butter in pan, add livers,

saute until browned on all sides. In separate pan, melt remaining 45g (1½oz) butter. Saute peeled and chopped onions and chopped bacon until onion is transparent. Add thyme, bayleaf and the livers, simmer further 5 minutes. Remove from heat, remove bayleaf. Put mixture with sherry in electric blender, blend until smooth. Fold in cream and extra melted butter, season with salt and pepper, allow mixture to cool. Spread evenly over gelatine mixture, refrigerate until firm. Unmould on to plate. Serves 6 to 8.

ITALIAN ANCHOVY PATE

2 x 60g (2oz) cans anchovy fillets
3 egg yolks
3 tablespoons lemon juice
salt, pepper
⅓ cup oil
1 cup cream
½ stick celery
½ tomato
4 black olives
¼ red pepper
¼ green pepper
2 shallots
2 tablespoons bottled french dressing

Put undrained anchovy fillets into electric blender. Add egg yolks and lemon juice, blend on medium speed until combined. Gradually add oil in thin stream, blend on medium speed until thick and creamy. Add cream, blend until just combined. Season with salt and pepper. Pour into serving dish, refrigerate until firm. Put chopped celery, chopped tomato, seeded and chopped red and green peppers, chopped shallots, chopped olives and french dressing into bowl, toss lightly. Just before serving, spoon vegetable mixture over anchovy pate. Serve with drinks, with crusty bread. Serves 4 to 6.

TARAMASALATA

100g can tarama
⅓ cup lemon juice
½ cup oil
¼ teaspoon dried dill

Chicken liver pate.

Pates & Dips

salt, pepper
4 thick slices white bread
warm water
250g (8oz) potatoes
6 shallots

Place tarama, lemon juice and dill in electric blender, blend on medium speed until smooth. Gradually add oil in thin stream, blend until thick and smooth. Remove crusts from bread, put bread in bowl, cover with warm water, let stand 5 minutes. Put bread into strainer, press out as much water as possible. Gradually add bread to mixture in blender, blend until smooth. Peel and quarter potatoes, place in boiling salted water, boil until tender, drain. Mash potatoes well. Put potatoes into bowl, gradually beat in tarama mixture. Season with salt and pepper. Add chopped shallots, mix well. Spoon into serving dish. Refrigerate until ready to serve with drinks. Serves 8.

Note: Tarama is fish roe and it is available in small cans from most Continental food stores. In addition to the name tarama, it is labelled "red caviar" on the can.

EASY HOMMUS

2 x 315g (10oz) cans baby butter beans
½ cup tahini
2 teaspoons sesame oil
salt, pepper
2 cloves garlic
¼ cup lemon juice
2 tablespoons finely chopped chives or shallots
1 stick celery
¼ cup oil
1 tablespoon lemon juice, extra
2 tablespoons chopped mint
¼ teaspoon paprika

Drain butter beans, rinse under cold running water. Place beans into electric blender, add tahini, sesame oil, salt, pepper, crushed garlic and lemon juice, blend on medium speed until smooth. Mixture should be of a thick paste consistency; if too thick, add a little water and blend again. Remove from blender, add chives or shallots and

finely chopped celery, mix well. Spoon mixture into serving bowl. Combine oil, extra lemon juice, mint and paprika in bowl, allow to stand 15 minutes. Spoon over bean mixture, cover bowl, refrigerate until ready to serve. Serves 6.

Note: This is a quick and delicious version of Hommus, in which canned butter beans replace the more traditional garbanzos or chick peas, which need hours of cooking. Tahini (sesame paste) is available in cans from health food stores.

SMOKED SALMON DIP

250g (8oz) packaged cream cheese
1 cup sour cream
¼ cup mayonnaise
2 x 90g (3oz) cans smoked salmon
½ teaspoon grated lemon rind
2 teaspoons lemon juice
2 teaspoons french mustard
4 shallots
2 tablespoons chopped parsley
salt, pepper

Beat cream cheese until smooth, add sour cream and mayonnaise, beat until smooth. Fold in drained, chopped salmon, lemon rind, lemon juice, mustard, chopped shallots and parsley, mix well. Season with salt and pepper. Refrigerate until needed. Serves 6.

FRENCH ASPARAGUS DIP

250g (8oz) packaged cream cheese
½ cup sour cream
¼ cup mayonnaise
470g (15oz) can green asparagus tips
2 teaspoons curry powder
½ packet french onion soup mix
2 teaspoons lemon juice
2 tablespoons chopped parsley
1 teaspoon prepared mustard
salt, pepper

Beat cream cheese, sour cream and mayonnaise until smooth. Drain asparagus (reserve ¼ cup asparagus liquid). Chop asparagus, add to cream cheese mixture with reserved liquid, curry powder, dry soup mix, lemon juice, parsley and mustard, season with

salt and pepper. Refrigerate at least 1 hour before serving. Serves 6.

CURRIED EGG DIP

250g (8oz) packaged cream cheese
½ cup mayonnaise
½ cup sour cream
3 rashers bacon
1 small onion
30g (1oz) butter
1 teaspoon curry powder
½ teaspoon dry mustard
½ teaspoon paprika
salt, pepper
3 hard-boiled eggs
1 tablespoon chopped parsley

Beat cream cheese until soft and creamy, add mayonnaise and sour cream, beat until smooth. Heat butter in frying pan, add finely chopped bacon and peeled and finely chopped onion, saute gently until onion is tender and bacon is crisp, allow to cool. Add to cream cheese mixture the curry powder, mustard, paprika, cold onion mixture, shelled and finely chopped eggs and parsley, mix well. Season with salt and pepper. Refrigerate until ready to serve. Serves 6 to 8.

CHEESE DIP

125g (4oz) butter
2 teaspoons prepared mustard
½ cup mayonnaise
125g (4oz) cheddar cheese
1 tablespoon lemon juice
salt, pepper

Cream butter until light and fluffy, add mustard, mayonnaise, grated cheese, lemon juice, salt and pepper; beat for 3 minutes. Serve as a dip or serve with an assortment of fresh, crisp vegetables as first course for a dinner party. To do this, spoon dip into four small bowls set on individual plates. As accompaniments we used thin wedges of tomato, halved hard-boiled eggs, thin sticks of celery and cucumber, salami slices, black olives and crisp lettuce leaves. Use a small knife to spread the dip on to the accompaniments. Serves 4.

Italian anchovy pate.

Fish & Shellfish

Fish, an excellent protein food, should be added to the family menu once or twice a week. It also makes a delicious entree or main course for a dinner party

SOUFFLE OYSTERS
12 oysters on the shell
3 rashers bacon
60g (2oz) butter
1½ tablespoons plain flour
½ cup milk
1 teaspoon prepared mustard
60g (2oz) cheddar cheese
salt, pepper
2 eggs, separated

Put oysters on to baking tray. Remove rind from bacon, chop bacon into small pieces. Put in frying pan, cook until crisp: sprinkle evenly over oysters. Heat butter in pan, add flour, stir until combined, remove from heat. Gradually add milk, stir until combined. Add mustard, salt and pepper. Return pan to heat, stir until sauce boils and thickens, remove from heat. Add grated cheese and egg yolks, stir until combined. Allow mixture to cool until warm. Beat egg whites until soft peaks form, fold gently into cheese mixture. Spoon heaped teaspoonfuls of mixture on to each oyster. Bake in hot oven 5 minutes or until puffed and golden. Serve immediately. Serves 2.

BRAISED PRAWNS WITH MUSHROOMS
500g (1lb) green king prawns
250g (8oz) can bamboo shoots
250g (8oz) broccoli
470g (15oz) can straw mushrooms
1 tablespoon oil
½ cup chicken stock
1 teaspoon cornflour
1 teaspoon oyster sauce
salt, pepper
pinch sugar
½ teaspoon grated green ginger

Shell and de-vein prawns, sprinkle with salt. Drain bamboo shoots, cut into thin slices. Cut broccoli into thick pieces. Drain mushrooms. Heat oil in pan, saute prawns quickly until tender. Add bamboo shoots, broccoli and mushrooms, mix well. Blend cornflour with chicken stock, add to pan with oyster sauce, salt, pepper, sugar and ginger. Bring to boil, stirring, cook 1 to 2 minutes. Serves 4.

Note: If straw mushrooms are not available, replace them with canned champignons (small whole mushrooms).

SALMON AND ASPARAGUS PANCAKES
250g (8oz) can red salmon
470g (15oz) can green asparagus spears
3 hard-boiled eggs
salt, pepper
5 pancakes (see Index for recipe)
2 tablespoons chopped parsley
HOLLANDAISE SAUCE
3 egg yolks
185g (6oz) butter
1 tablespoon lemon juice
2 teaspoons white vinegar
½ teaspoon curry powder
salt, pepper

Remove skin and bones from salmon, put salmon in bowl, season with salt and pepper. Drain asparagus, slice eggs. Divide salmon equally on centre of each pancake, top with 4 asparagus spears, then arrange sliced egg over asparagus; roll up. Put pancakes on greased oven trays, bake in hot oven 5 minutes or until heated through. Spoon prepared Hollandaise Sauce over, then sprinkle with chopped parsley.

Hollandaise Sauce: Put egg yolks in

Parmesan crumbed fish.

Fish & Shellfish

top of double saucepan, add lemon juice, vinegar and curry powder, stir until combined. Add softened butter; mix well. Stand saucepan over simmering water, stir until butter melts and mixture thickens. Remove from heat immediately. Season with salt and pepper. Serves 5 as an entree.

SEAFOOD PANCAKES
500g (1lb) small prawns
1 bottle oysters (about 10 oysters)
125g (4oz) can crab
1 cup water
½ cup dry white wine
1 small onion
60g (2oz) butter
3 tablespoons plain flour
½ cup cream
salt, pepper
3 shallots
30g (1oz) butter, extra
2 tablespoons chopped parsley
3 tablespoons packaged dry bread-crumbs
60g (2oz) cheddar cheese
4 pancakes (see Index for recipe)

Shell prawns, remove back vein; reserve prawn shells. Drain oysters, remove sinews from crab. Put reserved prawn shells, water, wine and peeled and chopped onion in saucepan, bring to boil, reduce heat. Simmer uncovered 5 minutes; drain, reserve stock. (You will need 1 cup of the prawn stock). Heat butter in separate saucepan, add flour, stir until combined, remove pan from heat. Gradually add reserved cup of prawn stock, add cream, stir until combined. Return pan to heat, stir until sauce boils and thickens. Reduce heat, simmer, uncovered, 3 minutes; remove pan from heat. Heat extra butter in separate pan, add chopped shallots, saute 1 minute, add seafood, stir until combined. Add seafood mixture to sauce, mix well. Season with salt and pepper. Spoon filling down centre of each pancake, then roll up. Place on greased oven tray. Sprinkle over combined parsley, breadcrumbs and grated cheese. Bake in hot oven 5 minutes or until heated through. Serves 2 as main course or 4 as an entree. A small green salad of crisp lettuce leaves tossed in french dressing would be a nice accompaniment.

PRAWN COCKTAIL
750g (1½lb) small prawns
lemon slices or wedges
½ lettuce
4 shallots
2 tablespoons chopped parsley
BRANDY COCKTAIL SAUCE
⅓ cup tomato sauce
1 tablespoon tomato paste
2 teaspoons lemon juice
1 teaspoon white vinegar
few drops tabasco sauce
1 tablespoon brandy
salt, pepper
½ cup cream

Shell prawns, remove back veins. Wash prawns and pat dry. Put finely shredded lettuce, chopped shallots and parsley into bowl; toss lightly. Put lettuce mixture at base of 4 individual scallop shells or dishes, top' with prawns, cover, leave in refrigerator until ready to serve. On serving, spoon sauce over, serve with lemon wedges.

Brandy Cocktail Sauce: Put tomato sauce, tomato paste, lemon juice, vinegar, tabasco sauce, brandy, salt and pepper into bowl; mix well. Beat cream until soft peaks form, gently fold into tomato mixture. Serves 4 to 6.

COQUILLES SAINT-JACQUES
500g (1lb) scallops
125g (4oz) mushrooms
6 shallots
1 tablespoon chopped parsley
1 cup water
1 cup dry white wine
1 teaspoon lemon juice
60g (2oz) butter
3 tablespoons flour
2 egg yolks
1 cup cream
salt, pepper
60g (2oz) butter, extra
2 cups fresh breadcrumbs

Wash scallops, clean away any brown sections. Peel and thinly slice mushrooms, finely chop shallots. Put scallops, shallots, mushrooms, parsley, water, wine and lemon juice into pan. Bring slowly to boil; reduce heat, simmer very gently for 2 minutes or until scallops are just cooked. Overcooking will toughen them. Strain scallop mixture, reserve liquid. Put reserved liquid into pan, bring to boil,

boil uncovered until liquid is reduced by half. (You will need 1 cup of liquid). Melt butter in pan, add flour, stir until combined, remove pan from heat. Add reserved liquid, stir until combined. Return pan to heat, stir until sauce boils and thickens. Mix cream into lightly beaten egg yolks, gradually add to hot sauce. Stir further 1 minute, remove from heat. Add drained scallop mixture to hot sauce, season with salt and pepper. Spoon evenly into scallop shells or ovenproof dishes. Put on to oven tray. Melt extra butter in pan, add breadcrumbs, stir until combined and golden brown. Sprinkle evenly over scallops. Bake in moderate oven 15 to 20 minutes or until golden brown and heated through. Serves 4.

CURRIED CREAM PRAWNS
1kg (2lb) small prawns
60g (2oz) butter
1 large onion
1 clove garlic
1 tablespoon curry powder
3 tablespoons plain flour
3 cups water
3 chicken stock cubes
½ green apple
1 small banana
salt, pepper
2 tablespoons tomato sauce
1 tablespoon vinegar
¼ cup sour cream
2 cups fresh white breadcrumbs
60g (2oz) butter, extra

Shell prawns, remove back vein. Heat butter in pan, add peeled and finely chopped onion and crushed garlic, saute gently until onion is golden brown. Add flour and curry powder, stir 2 minutes, remove pan from heat. Add water, stir until combined. Return pan to heat, stir until sauce boils and thickens. Add crumbled stock cubes, peeled and finely chopped apple, chopped banana, salt, pepper, tomato sauce and vinegar; reduce heat, simmer covered 30 minutes. Remove lid from pan, simmer a further 15 minutes or until sauce is thick. Press mixture through sieve, return to pan, add prawns and cream, simmer for 2 minutes. Pour into ovenproof dish. Melt extra butter in pan, add breadcrumbs, stir until combined. Sprinkle over

Braised prawns with mushrooms.

prawns. Bake in hot oven 5 minutes or until crumbs are golden. Serves 4.

OYSTERS EN BROCHETTE
1 large bottle fresh oysters (approximately 30 oysters)
flour
salt, pepper
1 egg
2 cups fresh breadcrumbs
2 tablespoons chopped parsley
4 shallots
oil for deep-frying
SEAFOOD SAUCE
3 tablespoons tomato sauce
¼ teaspoon grated lemon rind
2 teaspoons lemon juice
¼ teaspoon worcestershire sauce
1 teaspoon french mustard
few drops tabasco sauce
½ cup cream
TURMERIC RICE
¾ cup rice
1 teaspoon turmeric
water

Drain oysters. Combine breadcrumbs, parsley and finely chopped shallots. Divide oysters between eight thin skewers. Gently push oysters on to skewers. Roll oysters on skewers in flour seasoned with salt and pepper. Coat in beaten egg, then with breadcrumb mixture. Put in deep hot oil, fry quickly 1 minute or until breadcrumbs are light golden brown. Drain on absorbent paper. Serve with Seafood Sauce, Turmeric Rice and a wedge of lemon.

Seafood Sauce: Put tomato sauce, lemon rind, lemon juice, worcestershire sauce, mustard and tabasco sauce into bowl; mix well. Beat cream until soft peaks form, lightly fold into tomato sauce mixture. Cover, refrigerate until ready to serve.

Turmeric Rice: Gradually add the rice to large quantity of boiling salted water. Add turmeric, boil uncovered 12 minutes or until rice is tender; drain well. Serves 4.

Note: Large bottles of oysters containing about 30 oysters are available at most large food stores. If not able to buy these, you will need three to four small bottles of oysters.

PARMESAN CRUMBED FISH

750g (1½lb) fish fillets
3 cups fresh breadcrumbs
1 tablespoon chopped parsley
2 tablespoons grated parmesan cheese
salt, pepper
1 teaspoon dry mustard
1 egg
2 tablespoons milk
flour
125g (4oz) butter
MUSTARD SAUCE
2 egg yolks
½ cup sour cream
1 teaspoon flour
½ cup milk
2 teaspoons prepared mustard
4 shallots

Remove skin from fillets. Combine breadcrumbs, parsley, parmesan and dry mustard, season with salt and pepper. Coat fish fillets with flour, dip into combined beaten egg and milk, coat well with breadcrumb mixture. Melt butter in large pan, fry fillets until

golden brown and cooked through. Serve with prepared Mustard Sauce.

Mustard Sauce: Mix flour to a smooth paste with a little of the milk. Combine with remaining milk, beaten egg yolks, sour cream, prepared mustard and chopped shallots; mix well. Pour into top of double saucepan. Stir over simmering water until thickened, remove from heat immediately. Serves 4 to 6.

CRISP-FRIED FISH PUFFS

750g (1½lb) fish fillets
3 slices bread
½ cup milk
1 teaspoon curry powder
1 tablespoon flour
1 egg
salt, pepper
1 egg, extra
2 tablespoons milk, extra
flour
packaged dry breadcrumbs
oil for deep-frying

Remove skin and bones from fillets, chop fish finely. Break up bread roughly, cover with milk, let stand 20 minutes. Combine chopped fish, soaked bread and milk, curry powder, flour, egg, salt and pepper; mix well. Refrigerate 1 hour. Form mixture into balls, coat with flour, then combined beaten extra egg and extra milk, then

coat well with breadcrumbs. Refrigerate 30 minutes. Deep-fry in hot oil until golden brown and cooked through. Makes approximately 35. Serve hot with Curry Sauce.

Curry Sauce: Melt 30g (1oz) butter in pan, add 1 tablespoon flour and 2 teaspoons curry powder, stir until smooth. Cook 1 minute, remove pan from heat, add 1 cup milk gradually, stir until smooth. Return pan to heat, stir until sauce boils and thickens. Add ¼ cup sour cream, 1 tablespoon chopped parsley, salt and pepper.

TROUT WITH WINE CREAM SAUCE

4 medium-sized trout
4 rashers bacon
flour
salt, pepper
60g (2oz) butter
¼ cup oil
½ cup mayonnaise
1 cup dry white wine
2 teaspoons french mustard
¾ cup sour cream
90g (3oz) slivered almonds
6 shallots

Wash and scale trout. Remove rind from bacon, cut bacon into small pieces. Put bacon into frying pan, cook gently until crisp; remove from pan. To fat in pan add slivered almonds, cook until golden brown; drain on absorbent paper. Chop shallots, combine with almonds and bacon. Coat trout lightly with flour seasoned with salt and pepper. Heat butter and oil in large frying pan, add trout, cook gently until golden brown and cooked through on both sides; keep warm. Drain fat from pan, leaving 2 tablespoons. Add wine and mustard, bring to boil, boil uncovered until liquid is reduced by half, remove pan from heat. Add mayonnaise and sour cream, stir until combined. Return pan to heat, stir until sauce boils, reduce heat, simmer for 1 minute. Season with salt and pepper. Put trout on serving plates, spoon sauce over, top with bacon mixture. Serves 4.

Left: Coquilles Saint-Jacques.
Right: Seafood pancakes.

HAWAIIAN FISH

750g (1½lb) fish fillets
1 tablespoon curry powder
1 teaspoon soy sauce
¼ teaspoon chilli powder
salt, pepper
2.5cm (1in) piece green ginger
470g (15oz) can pineapple slices
flour
2 eggs
2 tablespoons milk
packaged dry breadcrumbs
oil for deep-frying
½ red pepper
6 shallots
60g (2oz) butter

Remove skin from fish. Drain pineapple, reserve syrup. Put reserved pineapple syrup, curry powder, soy sauce, chilli powder, salt, pepper and peeled and grated green ginger into bowl; mix well. Add fish, let stand 1 hour. Drain fish, reserve liquid. Coat fish with flour, then dip in combined beaten eggs and milk. Coat fish firmly with breadcrumbs. Put into deep hot oil, fry fish until golden brown and cooked through; keep warm. Heat butter in pan, add reserved liquid, stir until combined. Add pineapple slices, seeded and sliced red pepper and chopped shallots, simmer uncovered for 3 minutes. Put fish on to serving plate, spoon over pineapple mixture. Serves 4.

TUNA CASSEROLE

1 onion
2 sticks celery
470g (15oz) can tuna
315g (10oz) can cream of celery soup
½ teaspoon grated lemon rind
2 tablespoons lemon juice
2 tablespoons chopped parsley
salt, pepper
315g (10oz) can whole kernel corn
packaged dry breadcrumbs
1 cup fresh breadcrumbs
30g (1oz) butter

Peel and grate onion, chop celery. Put in bowl with drained flaked tuna, undiluted soup, lemon rind and juice, parsley, salt, pepper and drained corn; mix well. Grease an ovenproof dish, dust lightly with dry breadcrumbs. Spoon tuna mixture into dish. Toss fresh breadcrumbs in melted butter, sprinkle over top. Bake in moderate oven 25 to 30 minutes. Serves 4.

CREAMY SALMON BALLS

250g (8oz) packet cream cheese
250g (8oz) can red salmon
1 teaspoon grated lemon rind
1 egg
salt, pepper
2 tablespoons mayonnaise
¼ cup sour cream
¼ teaspoon chilli powder
4 shallots
1 cup fresh white breadcrumbs
flour
oil for deep-frying
BATTER
⅓ cup plain flour
½ teaspoon salt
1 teaspoon baking powder
⅓ cup cornflour
½ cup milk

Beat cheese until soft and creamy. Add undrained salmon with bones removed, lemon rind, egg, salt, pepper, mayonnaise, sour cream, chilli powder, finely chopped shallots and breadcrumbs; mix well. Refrigerate until firm. Take tablespoons of mixture, roll into balls. Roll in flour seasoned with salt and pepper. Dip in prepared batter, put into deep hot oil, cook until golden brown; drain on absorbent paper.

Batter: Sift dry ingredients into bowl, make well in centre, gradually add milk, mix to a smooth batter.

TUNA RICE SLICE

1 cup rice
1 small onion
1 egg
30g (1oz) butter
500g (1lb) can tuna
60g (2oz) butter, extra
3 tablespoons flour
2 cups milk
1 teaspoon dry mustard
1 teaspoon paprika
60g (2oz) cheddar cheese
salt, pepper
2 tablespoons chopped parsley
1 egg, extra
2 teaspoons lemon juice

Gradually add rice to large saucepan of boiling salted water, boil uncovered for 12 minutes or until rice is tender; drain. Combine rice, egg, peeled and finely chopped onion and melted butter; mix well. Press over base and sides of well greased 18cm by 28cm (11in by 7in) lamington tin. Drain tuna, reserve liquid. Press flaked tuna over rice, pressing down firmly. Melt extra butter in pan, add flour, stir until combined, remove pan from heat. Add milk and reserved liquid, stir until combined. Return pan to heat, stir until sauce boils and thickens. Add mustard, paprika, salt and pepper, stir until combined, simmer uncovered for 2 minutes. Add well-beaten extra egg, grated cheese, parsley and lemon juice; stir until combined. Pour sauce over tuna. Bake uncovered in moderate oven for 40 minutes or until top is firm. Serves 6.

HOT AVOCADO WITH CRAB

2 ripe avocados
2 teaspoons lemon juice
salt, pepper
2 shallots
250g (8oz) frozen crab or 250g (8oz) can of crab
¼ cup grated parmesan cheese
SAUCE
30g (1oz) butter
1½ tablespoons flour
½ cup cream
½ cup milk
1 tablespoon tomato puree
¼ teaspoon curry powder
1 tablespoon mayonnaise

Cut avocados in half lengthwise, remove stones. Sprinkle each half with lemon juice, season with salt and pepper. Spoon thawed or drained crab evenly into each avocado half, sprinkle with chopped shallots. Spoon sauce evenly over crab, then sprinkle with parmesan cheese. Place avocados in baking dish in 2.5cm (1in) hot water. Bake in moderate oven 10 minutes or until cheese is golden. Serves 4.

Sauce: Melt butter in saucepan, add flour, stir until combined. Remove from heat, gradually add cream and milk; return to heat, stir until mixture boils and thickens. Reduce heat, add tomato puree, curry powder, mayonnaise, salt and pepper. Simmer 2 minutes, cool.

Hot avocado with crab.

Beef

For grills, casseroles or curries it is hard to beat the good flavour of beef. Try these favourite recipes

BEEF CURRY

1kg (2lb) topside or round steak
60g (2oz) butter
1 onion
30g (1oz) butter, extra
2 cooking apples
2 medium bananas
2 tablespoons curry powder
4 tablespoons flour
3 cups water
1 beef stock cube
1 tablespoon brown sugar
salt, pepper

Trim excess fat from meat, cut into 2.5cm (1in) cubes. Melt butter, brown meat well, remove from pan. Peel and finely chop onion, add to pan with extra butter, cook 1 minute. Peel and finely dice apples and bananas, add to pan with curry powder, cook 2 minutes. Add flour, stir 1 minute. Add water and crumbled stock cube, brown sugar, salt and pepper. Continue stirring until sauce boils and thickens; add meat; reduce heat, simmer, covered, 1 hour or until meat is tender. Serves 4 to 6.

GLAZED MEATLOAVES

500g (1lb) minced steak
500g (1lb) sausage mince
1 onion
2 eggs
1 tablespoon prepared mustard
1 tablespoon worcestershire sauce
1 tablespoon tomato sauce
2 sticks celery
½ cup fresh breadcrumbs
60g (2oz) butter
SAUCE
1 tablespoon flour
470g (15oz) can tomato soup
1 beef stock cube
¾ cup water
1 tablespoon soy sauce

Combine minced steak, sausage mince, finely chopped onion, lightly beaten eggs, mustard, worcestershire sauce, tomato sauce, finely chopped celery and breadcrumbs, mix well. Divide mixture evenly into four, shape into four separate loaves. Melt butter in baking dish, add meatloaves, bake in moderately hot oven 35 to 40 minutes or until well browned, turning once and basting frequently with pan juices. Remove from oven, put meatloaves in heatproof dish and keep warm in oven.

Sauce: Pour off excess fat from baking dish, add flour, cook until lightly browned. Add remaining ingredients, stir well; stir until sauce boils, reduce heat, simmer 2 minutes. Return meatloaves to baking dish, reduce heat to moderate, cook further 15 minutes, basting with the sauce. Serves 4.

SPICY CURRIED MEATBALLS

750g (1½lb) minced steak
250g (8oz) sausage mince
1 tablespoon curry powder
salt, pepper
2 eggs
3 tablespoons fruit chutney
1 large onion
60g (2oz) butter
1 large onion, extra
2 tablespoons curry powder, extra
1 teaspoon paprika
2.5cm (1in) piece green ginger
1 clove garlic
2 teaspoons turmeric
2 tablespoons plain flour
2½ cups water
3 tablespoons tomato paste
3 tablespoons fruit chutney, extra
1 green apple

Put minced steak, sausage mince, curry powder, salt, pepper, eggs, fruit chutney and peeled and finely chopped onion into bowl; mix well. Roll tablespoonfuls of mixture into balls. Heat butter in pan, add a quarter of the meatballs, cook until golden brown, shaking pan constantly; remove meatballs from pan. Repeat with remaining meatballs. Add peeled and finely chopped extra onion, extra curry powder, paprika, peeled and grated ginger, crushed garlic and turmeric, saute gently until onion is tender. Add flour, stir until golden brown, add water, tomato paste, extra fruit chutney and peeled and grated apple, stir until sauce boils and thickens. Return meatballs to pan, season with salt and pepper. Cover pan, simmer gently 30 minutes or until meatballs are tender. Serves 6.

BEEF AND PEPPER CASSEROLE

1.25kg (2½lb) chuck steak
2 tablespoons flour
1 teaspoon salt
30g (1oz) butter
1 tablespoon oil
1 small red pepper
315g (10oz) can red kidney beans
SAUCE
470g (15oz) can whole tomatoes
½ cup dry red wine
1 tablespoon worcestershire sauce
2 tablespoons brown sugar
2 tablespoons white vinegar
1 clove garlic, crushed

Trim any surplus fat off meat, cut meat into 2.5cm (1in) cubes. Coat meat in combined flour and salt. Heat butter and oil, saute the meat until well browned. Transfer meat to casserole, pour over the sauce. Cook, covered, in moderate oven 2 hours or until meat is tender. Add sliced pepper and drained and rinsed kidney beans 30 minutes before end of cooking time.

Sauce: Combine undrained tomatoes with other ingredients. Serves 6.

Beef and mushroom casserole.

Beef

PEPPERED BEEF PUFFS

1kg (2lb) minced steak
3 eggs
½ cup packaged dry breadcrumbs
6 shallots
salt, pepper
black pepper
60g (2oz) butter
500g (1lb) pkt puff pastry
1 egg yolk
1 tablespoon water

MUSHROOM SAUCE

90g (3oz) butter
250g (8oz) button mushrooms
3 tablespoons flour
1 cup dry red wine
1½ cups water
2 beef stock cubes
½ teaspoon basil
3 tablespoons tomato paste
salt, pepper

Put meat, eggs, breadcrumbs, finely chopped shallots, salt and pepper into bowl; mix well. Divide meat into 6 equal portions. Shape into small loaves. Grind black pepper over loaves, pressing in lightly. Heat butter in frying pan, cook loaves on all sides until golden brown, remove from pan, cool. Cut pastry into 6 equal portions, roll out each portion to 23cm by 12cm (9in by 5in) rectangle. Put cold meatloaf into centre of each pastry strip, brush edges of pastry with combined egg yolk and water, roll up and secure ends firmly. Make 2 or 3 slits in top of pastry. Put on lightly greased oven tray. Brush each loaf with egg yolk mixture. Bake in hot oven 10 minutes or until golden, reduce heat to moderate, cook further 15 minutes. Serve sauce separately.

Mushroom Sauce: Heat butter in pan. Add finely sliced mushrooms, saute until mushrooms are tender. Add flour, stir until combined; cook 1 minute. Remove pan from heat, add wine, water and crumbled stock cubes. Return pan to heat, stir until sauce boils and thickens; season with salt and pepper. Add basil and tomato paste, mix well. Simmer sauce uncovered 5 minutes. Serves 6.

BEEF POT ROAST

90g (3oz) butter
2kg (4lb) piece of corner topside
3 large carrots
3 medium parsnips
8 small onions
4 medium potatoes
⅓ cup plain flour
1.25 litres (5 cups) water
3 beef stock cubes
3 tablespoons tomato paste
1 teaspoon worcestershire sauce
pinch mixed herbs
1 teaspoon sugar
salt, pepper

Heat 30g (1oz) butter in large pan, add meat, brown well on all sides. Remove meat from pan. Add to pan scraped carrots, cut into large pieces; scraped parsnips, cut into large pieces; peeled whole onions; and peeled potatoes cut in half. Saute gently until vegetables are golden brown. Remove from pan. Melt remaining butter in pan. Add flour, stir over high heat until flour is dark golden brown. Remove pan from heat, add water, stir until combined. Add crumbled stock cubes, tomato paste, worcestershire sauce, mixed herbs, salt, pepper and sugar. Return pan to heat, stir until sauce boils and thickens. Put meat into large saucepan, pour sauce over, bring to boil. Reduce heat, cover, simmer gently 2 hours. Add prepared vegetables, simmer further 30 minutes or until vegetables are tender. Keep meat and vegetables warm on serving plate. Bring sauce in pan to boil, boil uncovered 10 minutes or until of good gravy consistency. Serves 6.

HERBED BEEF

500g (1lb) minced steak
125g (4oz) bacon pieces
2 onions
470g (15oz) can tomato soup
1½ cups water
1 beef stock cube
½ teaspoon mixed herbs
salt, pepper

Peel and chop onions, dice bacon. Saute onions in pan until transparent, add bacon, saute further five minutes. Stir in steak, cook until meat browns; pour off any surplus fat. Add undiluted soup, water, crumbled stock cube, herbs, salt and pepper. Bring to boil, stirring; reduce heat, cover, simmer 20 to 25 minutes. Serve with rice or spaghetti. Serves 4.

CHINESE BEEF

1kg (2lb) rump steak
1 tablespoon soy sauce
salt, pepper
1 teaspoon curry powder
1 teaspoon ground ginger

Peppered beef puffs.

1 teaspoon bicarbonate of soda
1 teaspoon sugar
1 tablespoon dry sherry
1 tablespoon oil
2 tablespoons oil, extra
2 onions
1 red pepper
1 green pepper
1 tablespoon cornflour
1½ cups water
1 beef stock cube
1 teaspoon soy sauce, extra
2 teaspoons dry sherry, extra
½ teaspoon sugar, extra

Trim fat from meat, cut meat into 5cm (2in) squares; flatten well with meat mallet or rolling pin. Put meat in bowl with soy sauce, salt, pepper, curry

Chinese beef.

powder, ginger, bicarbonate of soda, sugar, sherry and oil. Mix well, allow to marinate at least 2 hours or, covered, overnight in refrigerator. Heat extra oil in large pan, add meat slices to pan, spreading slices out; do not allow slices to overlap; brown well on both sides, remove from pan. It may be necessary to do this in small quantities. Rinse and wipe pan, add peeled and quartered onions, cubed peppers, cornflour mixed with water, crumbled stock cube, extra soy sauce, sherry and sugar. Bring to boil, stirring. Cook 2 minutes or until vegetables are cooked but still crisp. Return meat slices to pan with meat juices, toss lightly until heated through. Serves 4.

BEEF AND MUSHROOM CASSEROLE
1.5kg (3lb) round steak
60g (2oz) butter
1 tablespoon oil
2 medium onions
30g (1oz) butter, extra
3 tablespoons flour
2 beef stock cubes
1 cup dry red wine
2 cups water
2 tablespoons tomato paste
salt, pepper
250g (8oz) mushrooms
sour cream

Remove fat and gristle from meat. Cut meat into 2.5cm (1in) pieces. Heat butter and oil in frying pan, add small quantity of meat to pan, brown well on all sides. Remove meat from pan, repeat process until all meat is well browned. Add peeled and sliced onions and sliced mushrooms to pan, saute gently for 3 minutes, remove from pan. Add extra butter and flour to pan, stir until flour is golden brown, remove pan from heat. Add wine, water, crumbled stock cubes, tomato paste, salt and pepper, stir until combined. Return pan to heat, stir until sauce boils and thickens. Return meat, onions and mushrooms to pan, bring to boil, reduce heat, simmer covered for 1½ hours or until meat is tender. Serve sour cream separately; a spoonful can be stirred into each serving Serves 6.

23

Lamb

Lamb is a flavour favourite with most families. Here is a range of recipes using the various cuts

ITALIAN CUTLETS

8 cutlets
2 tablespoons oil
1 large clove garlic
½ cup oil, extra
4 large potatoes
60g (2oz) butter
2 tablespoons lemon juice
2 tablespoons dry sherry
1 teaspoon basil
salt, pepper
2 tablespoons chopped parsley

Put cutlets on tray. Combine oil and crushed garlic in bowl, spoon over cutlets, let stand 2 hours. Peel potatoes, cut into 2.5cm (1in) cubes. Heat extra oil in large frying pan, add potatoes, fry until golden brown and cooked through, tossing potatoes frequently; drain, keep warm. Drain all oil from frying pan, add butter and cutlets, fry cutlets gently until golden brown and cooked through; remove from pan, keep warm. To remaining butter in pan add lemon juice, sherry, basil, salt, pepper and parsley, bring to boil, stirring constantly; remove pan from heat. Put cutlets on serving plate, add potatoes, spoon sauce over cutlets. Green beans make a good accompaniment. Serves 4.

MINTED RACKS OF LAMB

4 racks lamb (see below)
⅓ cup finely chopped mint
salt, pepper
½ cup vinegar
½ cup dry white wine
1 tablespoon sugar
60g (2oz) butter
2 tablespoons flour
½ cup dry white wine, extra
½ cup water
1 tablespoon sugar, extra

Have butcher cut four individual racks of lamb, each containing three to four cutlets in one piece; have him trim the bones well to give neat shape. Put racks into baking dish. Combine mint, salt, pepper, vinegar, white wine and one tablespoon sugar. Pour over lamb in baking dish. Bake in moderate oven 20 minutes, remove from oven, drain off liquid, reserve. Put butter in pan with lamb. Bake further 20 to 25 minutes or until lamb is cooked. Remove from pan, keep warm. Add flour to pan. Stir over low heat until golden brown, add extra white wine, water, extra sugar and reserved pan juices. Continue stirring until mixture boils and thickens. Roast potatoes, pumpkin and green peas are good accompaniments. Serve the mint gravy separately. Serves 4.

LAMB CURRY

90g (3oz) butter
2 x 1.25g (2½lb) legs lamb
3 large onions
3 cloves garlic
5cm (2in) piece green ginger
1 teaspoon cinnamon
1 teaspoon ground cardamom
2 teaspoons garam masala
2 tablespoons curry powder
2 x 200g cartons plain yoghurt
3 cups water
¼ cup tomato paste
salt, pepper
½ teaspoon chilli powder
¼ cup lemon juice
2 chicken stock cubes

Have butcher bone legs of lamb. Remove all fat from meat, cut meat into 2.5cm (1in) cubes. Heat butter in large frying pan, add meat, a few portions at a time; brown well on all sides, remove from pan, repeat with remaining meat. Put peeled and chopped onions, peeled garlic, peeled and chopped ginger, cinnamon, cardamom, garam masala, curry powder and chilli powder in electric blender, blend on medium speed 3 minutes or until mixture is a fine puree. Add to pan in which meat has been cooked, stir until onion mixture is very thick. Add yoghurt, water, crumbled stock cubes, salt, pepper, lemon juice and tomato paste, stir until combined. Return meat to pan, stir until combined. Bring to boil, reduce heat, simmer covered for 45 minutes. Remove lid, simmer a further 30 minutes or until meat is tender and sauce is very thick. Serves 4 to 6.

Note: Garam masala (Indian mixed spice) is available from large food stores or health food stores.

LAMB CHOP CASSEROLE

1kg (2lb) forequarter lamb chops
60g (2oz) butter
1 large onion
2 large carrots
2 large parsnips
30g (1oz) butter, extra
3 tablespoons flour
2½ cups water
3 tablespoons tomato sauce
1 teaspoon worcestershire sauce
2 tablespoons chopped parsley

Remove any excess fat from chops. Heat butter in frying pan, add chops, brown well on both sides; remove from pan. Add peeled and sliced onion, peeled and sliced carrots and peeled and sliced parsnips. Saute gently until onion is tender and golden brown; remove from pan. Melt extra butter in pan, add flour, stir until golden brown; remove pan from heat. Add water, tomato sauce and worcestershire sauce, stir until combined. Return pan to heat, stir until sauce boils and thickens, season with salt and pepper. Place chops and vegetables in ovenproof dish, pour sauce over. Bake, covered, in moderate oven 1 hour or until chops are tender. Just before serving, stir in chopped parsley. Serves 4 to 6.

Shoulder of lamb with vegetables.

Lamb

CRUMBED NOISETTES OF LAMB

8 lamb short loin chops
⅓ cup fruit chutney
2 teaspoons french mustard
salt, pepper
¼ teaspoon thyme
flour
dry breadcrumbs
4 eggs
60g (2oz) butter
3 tablespoons oil

MINT AND CHIVE BUTTER

125g (4oz) butter
3 tablespoons chopped mint
2 tablespoons chopped chives or shallots
1 tablespoon chopped parsley
salt, pepper

Ask butcher to cut each chop 3cm (approximately 1¼in) thick. Remove bones or ask butcher to do this for you. Combine sieved chutney, mustard, salt, pepper and thyme in bowl. Spread chutney mixture evenly over chops, then roll up each firmly into neat round; secure with small wooden skewer. Coat chops with flour seasoned with salt and pepper. Dip into beaten eggs, then coat firmly with breadcrumbs. Repeat egg-and-breadcrumb process. Put chops on to tray, refrigerate until ready to cook. Heat butter and oil in large frying pan. Put chops into pan, cook over very low heat until golden brown and cooked through, approximately 8 minutes each side. Drain on absorbent paper. Put on to serving plate, top each with a thick slice of Mint-and-Chive Butter.

Mint-and-Chive Butter: Put softened butter and remaining ingredients into bowl, mix well. With wet hands, form into roll approximately 2.5cm (1in) in diameter. Roll up in greaseproof paper, refrigerate until set and ready to serve.

CURRIED ONION CHOPS

750g (1½lb) lamb chops
45g (1½oz) butter
1 onion
1 apple
2 tablespoons flour
2 teaspoons curry powder
salt, pepper
½ teaspoon dry mustard
2 chicken stock cubes
2 cups boiling water
1 tablespoon worcestershire sauce

Saute chops in melted butter until golden brown, remove from pan. Peel and chop onion and apple, add to pan, saute until onion is transparent, remove from pan, drain. Add flour, curry powder, salt, pepper and mustard to pan, cook 3 minutes. Dissolve chicken stock cubes in boiling water, add worcestershire sauce, gradually add to flour mixture, stirring continually. Stir until sauce boils and thickens, reduce heat, simmer 3 minutes. Return chops, onion, apple to sauce, cover, simmer 1 hour or until chops are tender. Serves 4.

SHOULDER OF LAMB WITH VEGETABLES

1 shoulder lamb
2 cups fresh breadcrumbs
2 tablespoons chopped parsley
½ teaspoon sage or basil
60g (2oz) butter
1 egg
30g (1oz) butter, extra
3 tablespoons flour
1 cup water
1 beef stock cube
½ cup dry white wine
470g (15oz) can whole tomatoes
2 teaspoons soy sauce
¼ teaspoon sage, extra
4 large potatoes
500g (1lb) pumpkin
1 tablespoon chopped parsley, extra

Ask butcher to bone shoulder of lamb. Put breadcrumbs, parsley, sage or basil, melted butter and egg in bowl; season with salt and pepper, mix well. Put meat on board, skin side down, spread stuffing evenly over meat, roll up as for swiss roll. Tie securely with string. Heat extra butter in large saucepan, add lamb, cook until golden brown on all sides, remove lamb from pan. Pour off excess fat, leaving approximately 4 tablespoons of fat in pan. Add flour, stir until combined, cook 1 minute; remove pan from heat, gradually add water, add crumbled stock cube, extra sage and wine; stir until combined. Return pan to heat, stir until sauce boils and thickens. Add undrained tomatoes and soy sauce; stir until combined, season with salt and pepper. Strain sauce, pushing tomatoes through sieve. Return sauce to pan, add lamb, cover pan, simmer gently 1 hour. Add peeled and halved potatoes and peeled and seeded pumpkin, cut into pieces. Simmer gently a further 30 minutes or until vegetables are tender; stir in extra parsley. Serves 4 to 6.

DEVILLED LAMB CHOPS

1kg (2lb) best end lamb neck chops
1 tablespoon oil
½ cup water
3 teaspoons curry powder
1 teaspoon soy sauce
½ cup fruit chutney
salt, pepper
1 teaspoon dry mustard
1 tablespoon brown sugar

Put oil, water, curry powder, soy sauce, sieved fruit chutney, salt, pepper, mustard and brown sugar into large bowl; mix well. Add chops, mix well. Let stand at least 1 hour. Put chops in single layer in baking dish, spoon over any remaining sauce. Cover, bake in moderate oven 30 minutes. Remove cover and bake further 15 minutes, turning chops frequently. Serves 6.

NAVARIN OF LAMB

1.25kg (2½lb) boned shoulder of lamb
60g (2oz) butter
2 tablespoons oil
flour
1 clove garlic
3 beef stock cubes
2½ cups water
½ cup tomato puree
4 small turnips
12 small white onions
125g (4oz) bacon
30g (1oz) butter, extra
12 small potatoes
125g (4oz) peas
2 tablespoons chopped parsley

Cut meat into 2.5cm (1in) cubes, remove excess fat, toss in flour. Melt butter and oil in large pan, add meat and brown well, remove from pan. Add crushed garlic, saute 1 minute. Add 1 tablespoon flour to pan, cook 1 minute. Add water, crumbled stock cubes and tomato puree, stir until smooth and sauce boils, reduce heat, add meat, simmer covered 30 minutes. In separate pan, saute peeled onions and chopped bacon in extra melted butter 1 minute. Add to pan with peeled and sliced turnips, peeled potatoes and shelled peas. Bring back to boil, reduce heat, simmer covered further 30 to 35 minutes or until meat and vegetables are tender. Add parsley. Serves 4.

ROAST LAMB WITH PORT

2kg (4lb) shoulder lamb
60g (2oz) butter

Navarin of lamb.

½ cup port
2 tablespoons tomato sauce
1 tablespoon brown vinegar
½ teaspoon worcestershire sauce
2 tablespoons flour
2½ cups water
salt, pepper
2 tablespoons chopped mint
APPLE STUFFING
60g (2oz) butter
1 medium onion
1 clove garlic
2 rashers bacon
1 medium apple
2 tablespoons chopped parsley
2 cups fresh breadcrumbs

salt, pepper
1 egg

Ask butcher to bone shoulder of lamb. Spread lamb out on board, skin side down. Press prepared stuffing over lamb, coming to 2.5cm (1in) from edges. Roll up tightly. Tie with string at 2.5cm (1in) intervals. Put into baking dish, dot with butter. Bake in moderately hot oven 30 minutes, reduce heat to moderate, cook further 30 minutes. Combine ¼ cup port, tomato sauce, vinegar and worcestershire sauce, pour over lamb in baking dish. Bake further 30 minutes or until lamb is tender, basting frequently. Remove

lamb from baking dish; keep warm. Put baking dish over high heat on top of stove; when marinade has evaporated, remove pan from heat. Add flour, stir until combined, add water, stir until combined. Return pan to heat, stir until sauce boils and thickens. Reduce heat, simmer gently 10 minutes. Season with salt and pepper. Add remaining ¼ cup port and mint, simmer 2 minutes.

Apple Stuffing: Heat butter in pan, add peeled and chopped onion, crushed garlic, chopped bacon and peeled, cored and chopped apple. Saute gently 3 minutes. Add to remaining ingredients, mix well. Serves 6.

27

Veal

Veal, one of the tenderest of meats, is handy for the busy housewife and business woman; preparation is simple, cooking time is short

LEMON-CREAM VEAL
500g (1lb) veal steak
3 tablespoons lemon juice
3 tablespoons dry vermouth
2 tablespoons oil
salt, pepper
flour
2 eggs
1 cup packaged dry breadcrumbs
½ teaspoon grated lemon rind
2 tablespoons chopped parsley
chopped chives or shallot tops
60g (2oz) ground almonds
90g (3oz) butter
1 tablespoon oil, extra
½ cup cream
1 tablespoon chopped parsley, extra

Pound veal steaks out very thinly or ask butcher to do this. Cut veal steaks in half, remove any fat or gristle. Combine lemon juice, vermouth, oil, salt and pepper in bowl; add veal steaks, mix well, allow to stand 2 hours. Drain veal steaks, reserve marinade. Coat veal in flour seasoned with salt and pepper. Dip in beaten eggs, then coat veal in combined breadcrumbs, lemon rind, parsley, chives or shallots and almonds, pressing coating on firmly. Heat butter and extra oil in large frying pan, add veal, cook on both sides until golden brown and cooked through; remove from pan, keep warm. Add reserved marinade to butter mixture in pan, bring to boil, boil uncovered 1 minute. Add cream, stir until combined. Bring to boil, season with salt and pepper, remove from heat. Stir in extra parsley. Place veal on serving dish, pour sauce over. Serves 4.

VEAL CORDON BLEU
4 large veal steaks (or 8 smaller pieces)
4 small slices leg ham
4 slices swiss cheese
flour
salt, pepper
3 eggs
¼ cup milk
dry breadcrumbs
60g (2oz) butter
¼ cup oil

Cut each large veal steak in half. Pound out each piece very thinly. Trim edges to form oval shape. You will need two pieces of veal the same size to make one serving of Veal Cordon Bleu. Put a piece of ham, then a slice of cheese on each of four slices of veal, making sure filling comes to within 1cm (½in) of edge of veal all round. Top with remaining veal slices, pressing edges of veal together firmly. Coat veal lightly with flour seasoned with salt and pepper. Dip into combined beaten eggs and milk, then into breadcrumbs, pressing crumbs on firmly. Repeat egg-and-breadcrumbs process. Heat butter and oil in large frying pan. Add veal steaks. Cook gently on both sides until golden brown; approximately 6 minutes each side. Serves 4.

ITALIAN VEAL
4 veal steaks
1 egg
1 cup packaged dry breadcrumbs
salt, pepper
¼ teaspoon oregano
60g (2oz) butter
2 tablespoons oil
grated parmesan cheese
SAUCE
30g (1oz) butter
1 small onion
1 clove garlic
125g (4oz) mushrooms
470g (15oz) can whole tomatoes
salt, pepper
¼ teaspoon oregano
1 teaspoon sugar

Pound veal steaks out very thinly or ask butcher to do this. Dip steaks into beaten egg, then breadcrumbs seasoned with salt, pepper and oregano. Heat butter and oil in frying pan, add veal steaks, cook gently until golden brown on both sides and cooked through. Put on serving plate, top with sauce, then finely grated cheese.

Sauce: Heat butter in pan, add peeled and finely chopped onion and crushed garlic, saute gently until onion is tender. Add chopped mushrooms, saute 3 minutes. Add undrained, mashed tomatoes, salt, pepper, oregano and sugar. Bring to boil, reduce heat, simmer uncovered 10 minutes. Serves 4.

VEAL WITH ALMONDS
750g (1½lb) veal steak
¼ cup flour
2 eggs
1½ cups packaged dry breadcrumbs
⅓ cup grated parmesan cheese
90g (3oz) ground almonds
⅓ cup chopped parsley
¼ teaspoon thyme
1 clove garlic
salt, pepper
4 tablespoons oil
SAUCE
1 tablespoon brandy
½ cup dry white wine
½ cup cream
salt, pepper

Combine breadcrumbs, cheese, almonds, parsley, thyme, salt and pepper. Pound veal steaks very thinly, roll in flour, dip in beaten eggs, coat with breadcrumb mixture, pressing on firmly. Refrigerate 30 minutes to firm crumbs. Saute crushed garlic and steaks in hot oil, cook both sides until golden and cooked through. Remove from pan, keep warm while preparing sauce.

Sauce: Drain excess oil from pan, add brandy, wine, salt and pepper. Boil for a few minutes, stirring in all brown pan drippings. Remove from heat, stir in cream, reheat gently. Serves 4.

Veal and eggplant casserole.

Veal

VEAL AND EGGPLANT CASSEROLE

6 veal steaks
flour
salt, pepper
60g (2oz) butter
¼ cup oil
60g (2oz) butter, extra
½ cup dry white wine
2 medium eggplants
oil for shallow-frying
250g (8oz) mozzarella cheese
¼ cup grated parmesan cheese

TOMATO SAUCE
470g (15oz) can whole tomatoes
1 large onion
1 clove garlic
30g (1oz) butter
salt, pepper
¼ teaspoon oregano
½ teaspoon basil
2 tablespoons tomato paste
½ cup water
2 chicken stock cubes
½ teaspoon sugar

Pound veal out thinly, cut each steak in half. Coat veal with flour seasoned with salt and pepper. Heat butter and oil in frying pan until very hot. Add veal, a few pieces at a time, and cook very quickly on both sides until light golden brown. Remove from pan. Repeat with remaining veal. Place veal steaks in large shallow ovenproof dish in one layer. To pan drippings add wine, salt and pepper, bring to boil, stir until liquid is reduced by half. Remove from pan, add extra butter, stir until combined. Spoon wine mixture over veal. Spoon prepared Tomato Sauce evenly over veal. Cut eggplant into 1cm (½in) rounds. Coat each side lightly with flour seasoned with salt and pepper. Shallow-fry eggplant on each side for 1 minute in hot oil, drain. Overlap eggplant slices on Tomato Sauce. Cover eggplant with thin slices of mozzarella cheese, sprinkle over parmesan cheese. Bake in moderately hot oven for 30 minutes or until golden brown.

Tomato Sauce: Heat butter in pan, add peeled and finely chopped onion and crushed garlic, saute gently until onion is tender. Add undrained mashed tomatoes, salt, pepper, oregano, basil, tomato paste, water, crumbled stock cubes and sugar, stir until combined. Bring to boil, reduce heat, simmer uncovered for 20 minutes or until mixture is thick. Serves 4 to 6.

Lemon-cream veal.

SAVOURY VEAL CASSEROLE

125g (4oz) bacon pieces
60g (2oz) butter
3 tablespoons oil
1 large onion
2 large carrots
375g (12oz) potatoes
1 clove garlic
750g (1½lb) stewing veal
5 tablespoons flour
2 cups water
2 chicken stock cubes
½ teaspoon soy sauce
¼ teaspoon worcestershire sauce
¼ teaspoon mixed herbs
salt, pepper
1 tablespoon chopped parsley

Remove any rind and excess fat from bacon pieces, chop roughly. Heat butter and oil in pan, add peeled and sliced onion, peeled and chopped carrots, peeled and quartered potatoes, crushed garlic and bacon. Saute gently until onion is transparent, remove from pan. Cut veal into 2.5cm (1in) cubes, roll in 2 tablespoons of the flour, add to pan, saute until well browned. Add rest of flour, cook 2 minutes, stirring constantly. Add water, crumbled stock cubes, sauces, mixed herbs, salt and pepper, mix well. Combine meat mixture and onion mixture; mix well. Put into greased ovenproof dish. Bake, covered, in moderately slow oven 1½ hours or until meat is tender. Before serving, stir in parsley. Serves 4.

Chicken and veal Kiev.

CHICKEN AND VEAL KIEV
2 medium-sized whole chicken breasts
4 medium-sized veal steaks
2 eggs
flour
salt, pepper
3 cups fresh white breadcrumbs (about ½ loaf bread)
60g (2oz) butter
2 tablespoons oil
375g (12oz) mushrooms
BUTTER FILLING
125g (4oz) butter
salt, pepper
2 tablespoons chopped parsley
4 shallots
1 teaspoon french mustard
½ clove garlic
¼ teaspoon oregano
¼ teaspoon thyme

Remove skin from chicken breasts. Carefully remove chicken meat from bones, giving 4 individual pieces. Gently pound each chicken breast out to an oval shape. Remove any fat or gristle from veal, pound veal out thinly, trim to size of chicken breasts. Divide butter filling evenly over chicken breasts. Spread out butter filling to 1cm (½in) from edge of chicken. (Make sure there are no holes in chicken or veal or butter filling will come out during cooking). Brush edges with beaten eggs, put veal on top, press edges together firmly. Coat with flour seasoned with salt and pepper. Dip into beaten eggs, then coat with breadcrumbs. Press breadcrumbs on firmly. Refrigerate until ready to use. Heat butter and oil in pan, add whole mushrooms, saute gently until mushrooms are tender, season with salt, pepper. Remove mushrooms from pan; keep warm until ready to serve. Increase heat so that pan is very hot, add crumbed chicken-and-veal pieces; cook until golden brown on both sides, then reduce heat and cook further few minutes until cooked through.

Butter Filling: Beat butter until soft and creamy, add salt, pepper, parsley, finely chopped shallots, mustard, crushed garlic, oregano and thyme; mix well. Serves 4.

31

Pork

These recipes present pork in different and delicious new ways

PORK LOIN WITH ORANGE LIQUEUR SAUCE
1kg (2lb) loin of pork
2 teaspoons salt
oil
½ cup orange juice
½ cup water
1 chicken stock cube
2 tablespoons grand marnier
2 teaspoons cornflour
salt, pepper
ORANGE AND CELERY STUFFING
60g (2oz) butter
1 small onion
½ stick celery
¼ teaspoon rosemary
1 teaspoon grated orange rind
1 cup fresh breadcrumbs
salt, pepper
1 egg yolk

Order pork loin with long flap so that it holds stuffing securely. Ask butcher to remove bones from pork loin and score pork rind well. Open loin out on board, with rind side down. Put prepared stuffing along centre of pork, forming into roll. Tie pork securely with string at 2.5 cm (1in) intervals. Rub pork rind well with oil, then rub salt well into rind; this ensures crisp crackling. Place pork roll into lightly oiled baking dish. Bake in hot oven 20 minutes. Reduce heat to moderate, cook further 1½ hours or until pork is cooked through. Remove string; keep pork warm. Drain off all fat from dish, add combined orange juice, water, crumbled stock cube, grand marnier and cornflour to pan. Stir until sauce boils and thickens. Reduce heat, simmer, uncovered, 5 minutes. Season with salt and pepper; strain.

Orange and Celery Stuffing: Heat butter in pan, add peeled and finely chopped onion, finely chopped celery and rosemary. Saute gently until onion is tender. Remove pan from heat, add orange rind, stir until combined. Combine breadcrumbs, onion mixture and egg yolk; mix well. Season with salt and pepper. Serves 4.

PORK CHOPS WITH APPLE GRAVY
4 pork chops
30g (1oz) butter
2 tablespoons oil
1 onion
1 tablespoon flour
1 beef stock cube
230ml can (or 1 cup) apple juice
1 large green apple

Heat butter and oil in pan, add peeled and sliced onion; cook until onion is transparent, remove from pan. Add chops, cook until brown on both sides, remove from pan. Add flour to pan, cook 1 minute, stirring; add crumbled stock cube and apple juice, mix well, stir until sauce boils and thickens. Reduce heat, return chops and onion to pan. Peel apple, slice thickly, place one or two slices on top of each chop; cover, cook over low heat 15 to 20 minutes, or until chops are tender. Serves 4.

PORK SPARERIBS
1kg (2lb) pork spareribs
1 cup canned pineapple juice
1 tablespoon honey
1 tablespoon soy sauce
1 tablespoon lemon juice
2 tablespoons fruit chutney
1 tablespoon tomato sauce
2.5cm (1in) piece green ginger
2 teaspoons cornflour
2 tablespoons water

Put spareribs in saucepan, cover with water. Bring to boil, remove from heat, drain. Put in baking dish in single layer. Combine pineapple juice, honey, soy sauce, lemon juice, chutney, tomato sauce and finely chopped ginger. Pour over ribs, let stand at least 1 hour; drain and reserve marinade. Mix cornflour to smooth paste with water, add to reserved marinade, stir over heat until mixture boils and thickens. Put ribs on wire rack over baking dish; bake in moderate oven 30 to 35 minutes or until tender, brushing occasionally with the sauce. Serve with remaining sauce spooned over. Serves 3 to 4.

SWEET AND SOUR PORK
2 teaspoons sugar
3 tablespoons soy sauce
1 tablespoon dry sherry
1 egg yolk
1.25kg (2½lb) lean pork chops
cornflour
oil for deep-frying
1 large onion
8 shallots
1 red pepper
125g (4oz) small mushrooms
1 medium cucumber
2 sticks celery
3 tablespoons oil, extra
470g (15oz) can pineapple pieces
2 tablespoons tomato sauce
¼ cup vinegar
1 cup water
1 chicken stock cube
1½ tablespoons cornflour, extra

Mix together sugar, 1½ tablespoons soy sauce, the sherry and egg yolk, stir well. Cut meat into 2.5cm (1in) cubes, place into soy sauce mixture. Stir until well coated with marinade. Cover, leave 1 hour, stir occasionally. Drain meat from marinade, reserve liquid. Toss meat lightly in cornflour. Heat oil, cook meat until golden brown and cooked through, drain well. Peel and slice onion; chop shallots; slice pepper thickly, remove seeds; slice mushrooms and celery; cut unpeeled cucumber into quarters, lengthwise, cut out seeds, cut cucumber into medium-sized slices. Heat 3 tablespoons oil in large pan, add all the prepared vegetables, saute 3 minutes. Drain pineapple. Add pineapple syrup to pan with marinade from meat, remaining soy sauce, tomato sauce, vinegar and crumbled stock cube. Blend extra cornflour and water, add to pan, stir until sauce boils and thickens. Add pineapple pieces, season with salt and pepper. Add prepared pork, stir until combined. Serves 6.

Sweet and sour pork.

Sausages

Nothing looks quite as appetising as golden brown sausages sizzling in the pan. Here we present them as hearty family meals and cocktail snacks and give our best ever recipe for sausage rolls

SAUSAGES WITH ONION GRAVY

1 kg (2lb) thick pork sausages
1 tablespoon oil
2 large onions
3 tablespoons plain flour
2½ cups water
2 beef stock cubes
2 tablespoons tomato sauce
½ teaspoon worcestershire sauce
salt, pepper

Heat oil in frying pan, add sausages, cook until golden brown; remove from pan. Add peeled and chopped onions, cook until golden brown. Add flour, stir until golden brown, remove pan from heat. Add water, stir until combined. Return pan to heat, stir until sauce boils and thickens. Add crumbled stock cubes, tomato sauce, worcestershire sauce, salt and pepper, stir until combined. Reduce heat, add sausages, cover, simmer gently 30 minutes. Boiled or mashed potatoes and bottled red cabbage are excellent accompaniments. Simply heat the cabbage in its own liquid; half a small, peeled and finely chopped apple also can be cooked with the cabbage. Serves 4 to 6.

CURRIED SAUSAGES

30g (1oz) butter
750g (1½lb) thick beef sausages
2 medium onions
1 apple
1 banana
500g (1lb) potatoes
1½ tablespoons curry powder
470g (15oz) can condensed vegetable soup
1½ cups water
1 beef stock cube
2 tablespoons chopped parsley

Melt butter in pan, add sausages, cook until golden brown and cooked through. Remove from pan, drain off excess fat, leaving approximately 1 tablespoon fat in pan. Add peeled and finely chopped onions to pan, saute gently until onions are golden brown. Add peeled and chopped apple, peeled and chopped banana, peeled and cubed potatoes, saute for 2 minutes. Add curry powder, stir for 1 minute. Add vegetable soup, water, crumbled stock cube, season with salt and pepper. Bring to boil, reduce heat, simmer covered for 15 minutes or until potatoes are just cooked. Add sausages, simmer a further 10 minutes uncovered. Stir in parsley just before serving. Serves 4.

CRUNCHY SAUSAGE NIBBLES

500g (1lb) sausage mince
1 onion
1 stick celery
1 egg
2 tablespoons tomato paste
1 teaspoon prepared mustard
1 tablespoon worcestershire sauce
salt, pepper
½ cup flour
1 egg, extra
2 tablespoons milk
1 teaspoon mixed herbs
oil for deep-frying
3 cups fresh breadcrumbs

Combine sausage mince, peeled and finely chopped onion, finely chopped celery, egg, tomato paste, mustard, worcestershire sauce, salt and pepper; mix well. Take spoonfuls of mixture and roll into lengths about 5cm (2in) long. Roll in flour, then dip in combined beaten extra egg and milk, roll in combined breadcrumbs and mixed herbs. Deep-fry in hot oil until golden brown and cooked through, approximately 5 minutes. Makes approximately 35. Serve with drinks or as party nibbles.

SAUSAGE ROLLS

750g (1½lb) sausage mince
1 large onion
¼ teaspoon mixed herbs
salt, pepper

Sausage rolls.

Sausages with onion gravy.

4 thick slices white bread
warm water
2 x 375g (12oz) pkts puff pastry
1 egg yolk
1 tablespoon cold water

Put sausage mince, peeled and grated onion, mixed herbs, salt and pepper into bowl. Cut crusts from bread, put bread in separate bowl. Pour over enough warm water to cover, let stand 5 minutes. Drain off water, squeeze bread gently to extract water. Add bread to sausage mince mixture; mix well; (bread absorbs any excess fat in sausage mince and helps to prevent meat shrinking inside pastry when cooking). Have pastry at room temperature; cut each packet of puff pastry in half. Roll out each piece of pastry to 30cm (12in) square. Trim edges of each piece of pastry on three sides, leaving one side untrimmed. This untrimmed side will be cut off later when rolling sausage rolls. Put meat mixture into large piping bag that does not have tube attached. Pipe meat along edge of pastry, opposite untrimmed edge. Turn edge of pastry over filling, then turn again so that filling is enclosed completely in pastry. Cut along edge of pastry with sharp knife. Repeat with remaining filling and pastry. With back of knife flatten rolls slightly at 1cm (½in) intervals. Brush rolls with combined cold water and egg yolk. Cut rolls in 5cm (2in) pieces. Use first roll as guide for size of remaining rolls. Put rolls on greased tray, side by side, just touching lightly. Bake in hot oven 10 minutes, reduce heat to moderate, cook further 15 minutes. Makes approximately 24.

Poultry

Here are popular ways with chicken for family meals and superb main courses when you entertain — plus a praise-winning recipe for duck

ITALIAN CHICKEN CASSEROLE

1.5kg (3lb) chicken
5 small onions
1 clove garlic
60g (2oz) butter
470g (15oz) can whole tomatoes
1 cup dry red wine
½ teaspoon basil
salt, pepper

Melt butter in pan, add one finely chopped onion, crushed garlic and chicken. Cook until chicken is brown, turning often. Transfer to ovenproof dish. Add undrained tomatoes, wine, basil, peeled whole onions and salt and pepper. Cover, bake in moderate oven 40 minutes or until chicken is tender. Serves 4.

PINEAPPLE-CURRY CHICKEN

1.5kg (3lb) chicken (or chicken pieces)
⅓ cup oil
2 onions
1 clove garlic
¼ cup flour
1 tablespoon curry powder
¼ teaspoon chilli powder
2 cups water
470g (15oz) can unsweetened pineapple juice
2 chicken stock cubes
¼ cup tomato paste
salt, pepper
2 tablespoons chopped parsley
4 shallots

Joint chicken into serving-size pieces. Heat oil in pan, add chicken pieces; cook, turning occasionally, until chicken is well browned on all sides. Remove chicken from pan, reserve pan drippings. Place chicken in ovenproof dish. Add peeled and sliced onions and crushed garlic to reserved pan drippings, saute until onions are golden brown. Stir in flour, curry powder and chilli powder; cook, stirring, until flour is golden brown. Remove from heat. Add water, pineapple juice, crumbled stock cubes, tomato paste, salt and pepper, mix until smooth. Return to heat, stir until sauce boils and thickens. Remove from heat, pour over chicken. Bake, covered, in moderate oven 45 to 55 minutes or until chicken is tender. Stir in chopped shallots and chopped parsley. Serves 4.

LEMON CHICKEN

1.25kg (2½lb) chicken
2 tablespoons dry sherry
1 teaspoon grated green ginger
1 tablespoon lemon juice
1 teaspoon soy sauce
1 teaspoon sugar
3 shallots
1 tablespoon dry sherry, extra
2 tablespoons chicken stock
oil for deep-frying
LEMON SAUCE
1 cup chicken stock
salt, pepper
2 tablespoons sugar
¼ cup lemon juice
½ lemon
1 tablespoon cornflour
1 tablespoon water
4 lemon slices, extra

Wash and dry chicken, cut in half lengthways, then cut in half across to give four pieces; clean well. Combine in bowl sherry, ginger, lemon juice, soy sauce, sugar and chopped shallots. Add chicken pieces, mix well, marinate 2 hours. Drain chicken, reserve marinade. Put drained chicken pieces into deep hot oil. Fry very gently until golden brown and cooked through (approximately 10 to 12 minutes). Drain well on absorbent paper. Put chicken in pan, add reserved marinade, extra sherry and chicken stock. Cover, simmer gently 5 minutes, uncover to turn occasionally. Chop chicken into serving size pieces, spoon Lemon Sauce over, garnish with the extra lemon slices.

Lemon Sauce: Combine chicken stock, salt, pepper, sugar and lemon juice in saucepan. Remove rind from lemon; slice lemon thinly, add to pan. Bring to boil, reduce heat, simmer gently 5 minutes. Remove lemon slices. Blend cornflour with water, add to sauce, stir until boiling; reduce heat, stir 1 minute. Adjust flavour of sauce; it may need extra sugar, depending on tartness of lemons. Add extra lemon slices to sauce, heat through. Serves 4.

TARRAGON CHICKEN

4 chicken thighs
3 tablespoons flour
30g (1oz) butter
1 tablespoon oil
1 tablespoon grated lemon rind
1 tablespoon lemon juice
1 tablespoon tarragon
1 chicken stock cube
¾ cup water
1 egg yolk
2 tablespoons cream
salt, pepper

Coat chicken in flour. Heat butter and oil in pan, saute chicken until golden brown. Drain, place chicken in ovenproof dish. Combine lemon rind, lemon juice, tarragon, crumbled stock cube and water in pan; bring to boil,

Chicken and mushroom casserole.

pour over chicken. Bake, covered, in moderately slow oven 1¼ to 1½ hours or until chicken is tender. Remove chicken from pan, keep warm. Add lightly beaten egg yolk and cream to pan juices. Stir over low heat until sauce thickens. Season with salt and pepper. Spoon over chicken. Serves 2 or 4.

SWISS CHICKEN
4 whole chicken breasts
flour
salt, pepper
90g (3oz) butter
1 clove garlic
¾ cup dry white wine
1 teaspoon french mustard
½ cup cream
3 shallots

8 slices ham
8 slices swiss cheese

Carefully remove chicken meat from bones, giving eight individual pieces. Dust chicken breasts lightly with flour seasoned with salt and pepper. Heat butter in frying pan, add crushed garlic and chicken; saute gently until chicken is light golden brown. Add wine, bring to boil, reduce heat. Simmer covered 20 minutes or until chicken is tender; remove chicken from pan. Put a slice of ham on each piece of chicken, then top with a slice of cheese. Put on heatproof serving dish. Cook in moderate oven, uncovered, for 10 minutes or until cheese has melted. While chicken is in oven, bring liquid in pan to boil, boil uncovered until approximately half-cup liquid remains in pan. Reduce heat, add cream, chopped shallots and mustard; stir until combined. Season with salt and pepper. Pour sauce over chicken to serve. Serves 4.

CRUNCHY CHICKEN WINGS
500g (1lb) chicken wings
2 tablespoons soy sauce
2.5cm (1in) piece of green ginger
1 cup self-raising flour
1 tablespoon oil
salt, pepper
1 tablespoon grated green ginger, extra
6 shallots
1 cup water
oil for deep-frying

Cut chicken wings at wing joints, giving 3 pieces each. Put pieces in pan, add sufficient water just to cover wings, add soy sauce and peeled, sliced green ginger. Bring slowly to boil; reduce heat, simmer until cooked (approximately 25 minutes). Drain. Sift flour into bowl, add oil, salt, pepper, extra grated green ginger and finely chopped shallots. Gradually add water, beat until smooth. Dip cooled chicken in batter; drain off excess batter. Deep-fry in hot oil over low heat until golden. Serve with drinks.

COQ AU VIN
2 x 1kg (2lb) chickens or 2kg (4lb)
chicken pieces
125g (4oz) butter
125g (4oz) bacon pieces
12 tiny onions
salt, pepper
250g (8oz) mushrooms
1 clove garlic
½ cup flour
2 chicken stock cubes
3 cups water
¼ cup brandy
2 cups dry red wine
¼ teaspoon thyme
¼ teaspoon mixed herbs
1 bayleaf

Cut chickens into serving-size pieces. Heat 60g (2oz) butter in large pan, add peeled whole onions and diced bacon, cook until onions are light golden brown, remove from pan. Add chicken pieces to pan a few at a time, brown well on all sides, remove from pan, repeat with remaining chicken. Add sliced mushrooms and crushed garlic to

At left, Swiss chicken and, at right, Coq au vin.

pan, saute gently until mushrooms are just wilted. Remove from pan. Add remaining butter to pan drippings. When butter has melted, add flour, stir until golden brown. Remove pan from heat, add water, wine, brandy, crumbled stock cubes, salt, pepper, thyme, mixed herbs and bayleaf, stir until combined. Return pan to heat, stir until sauce boils and thickens. Place chicken, vegetables and sauce in large ovenproof dish. Cover, bake in moderate oven 45 minutes or until chicken is tender. Serves 6.

MAYONNAISE CHICKEN PANCAKES

1.5kg (3lb) chicken
½ cup undiluted canned cream of

chicken soup
⅓ cup mayonnaise
¼ cup cream
1 teaspoon lemon juice
salt, pepper
4 shallots
2 teaspoons curry powder
8 pancakes (see Index for recipe)
2½ cups stale white breadcrumbs
(approximately ½ loaf bread)
2 tablespoons chopped parsley
60g (2oz) butter
1 egg
2 tablespoons milk

Steam or boil chicken in usual way until tender; cool. Remove skin and bones from chicken, cut meat into small pieces. Put chicken meat, chicken soup, mayonnaise, cream, lemon juice, salt, pepper, chopped shallots and curry

powder into bowl; mix well. Divide mixture evenly between pancakes; roll up. Heat butter in frying pan, add breadcrumbs and parsley; toss well. Remove from heat. Combine egg and milk, carefully roll pancakes in egg mixture, then roll in breadcrumbs. Put pancakes on greased oven tray. Bake in moderately hot oven 15 minutes or until light golden brown. Serves 4.

MARSALA CHICKEN

60g (2oz) butter
1.25kg (2½lb) chicken pieces
flour
salt, pepper
2 onions
1 tablespoon grated green ginger
2 cups water

Poultry

2 chicken stock cubes
¼ cup marsala
¼ cup cream
2 tablespoons chopped parsley

Coat chicken pieces in flour seasoned with salt and pepper. Saute chicken in melted butter until well browned; remove from pan. Add peeled and finely chopped onions and ginger to pan, saute over low heat until onions are transparent. Add water, crumbled stock cubes and marsala, bring to boil, reduce heat, return chicken pieces to pan, cover; simmer, stirring occasionally, 45 minutes or until chicken is cooked. Remove chicken from pan, bring liquid to boil, stir until liquid has reduced slightly. Reduce heat, stir in cream and parsley, pour over chicken. Serves 4.

CHINESE CHICKEN

1.5kg (3lb) chicken
4 tablespoons tomato sauce
2 tablespoons soy sauce
1 tablespoon dry sherry
1 tablespoon white vinegar
¼ teaspoon chilli powder
1 clove garlic
2.5cm (1in) piece green ginger

Wash and dry chicken. Combine tomato sauce, soy sauce, sherry, vinegar, chilli powder, crushed garlic and peeled and grated green ginger; mix well. Add chicken, coat well with marinade. Allow to stand several hours or overnight in refrigerator. Next day place chicken in baking dish, pour over marinade. Cover dish with foil. Bake in moderate oven 1½ hours, remove foil, bake a further 30 minutes, brushing frequently with marinade. Serves 4 to 6.

FRENCH HERBED CHICKEN

1.25kg (3lb) chicken
90g (3oz) butter
2 tablespoons chopped parsley
2 tablespoons finely chopped shallots
1 teaspoon french mustard
½ teaspoon tarragon
salt, pepper
1 cup dry white wine
½ cup water
30g (1oz) butter, extra
1 chicken stock cube
½ cup cream
1 tablespoon cornflour
STUFFING
2½ cups fresh white breadcrumbs

1 egg
½ teaspoon thyme
2 tablespoons chopped parsley
60g (2oz) butter
2 rashers bacon
1 small onion

Take a teaspoon and, with rounded side up, gently ease down and over chicken breast, separating skin from meat; be careful not to break skin. Place butter in bowl, beat until soft and creamy, add parsley, shallots, mustard, tarragon, salt and pepper; mix well. With small spatula carefully spread butter mixture evenly over whole chicken breast under skin. Stuff chicken with prepared Stuffing, close cavity. Put chicken into baking dish, add wine, water, crumbled stock cube and extra butter. Bake uncovered in moderate oven for 1½ hours or until chicken is tender, basting frequently with pan juices. Remove chicken from baking dish. Put dish on top of stove, bring liquid to boil, boil uncovered for 2 minutes, remove pan from heat. Add combined cream and cornflour, stir until combined. Return to heat, stir until sauce boils and thickens, add salt and pepper. Serve sauce with chicken.

Stuffing: Heat butter in pan, add peeled and chopped onion and chopped bacon, saute gently until onion is tender. Combine breadcrumbs, egg, thyme, parsley, salt, pepper and onion mixture; mix well. Serves 4.

CHICKEN AND MUSHROOM CASSEROLE

1.5kg (3lb) chicken
60g (2oz) butter
1 tablespoon oil
470g (15oz) can cream of chicken soup
1 cup water
1 cup dry white wine
½ cup cream
1 tablespoon plain flour
250g (8oz) mushrooms
¼ teaspoon dried rosemary
salt, pepper
370g (15oz) can artichoke hearts
3 rashers bacon
2 tablespoons chopped parsley
6 shallots

Heat butter and oil in frying pan, add chicken pieces, cook gently until chicken is golden brown on all sides. Remove chicken from pan. Drain off half the fat in pan, add sliced mushrooms, saute gently for 2 minutes.

Add flour, stir until combined. Remove pan from heat. Add undiluted chicken soup, water and wine, stir until combined. Return pan to heat, stir until sauce boils and thickens. Stir in cream. Add salt, pepper and rosemary. Put chicken pieces into ovenproof dish, pour over sauce. Cover, bake in moderate oven 60 minutes or until chicken is tender. Add parsley, chopped shallots and drained artichoke hearts, stir until combined. Return to oven for a further 5 minutes. Remove rind from bacon, cut each rasher into 3, roll up, secure with small wooden skewers. Put under griller until crisp. Remove skewers, put rolls on top of casserole to serve. Serves 4.

DUCK WITH MANGOES

2 x 1.5kg (3lb) ducks
60g (2oz) butter
½ cup flour
2 cups water
1 cup dry white wine
2 tablespoons port
½ cup grand marnier
2 tablespoons brandy
½ cup orange juice
salt, pepper
500g can mango slices
1 bayleaf
pinch thyme

Wash and dry ducks, put into baking dish. Brush each duck with melted butter. Bake in moderately hot oven 60 minutes or until golden brown; brush ducks frequently with melted butter. Remove ducks from pan, drain all fat from pan; reserve fat. Put baking dish on top of stove, stand over high heat until pan drippings have turned golden brown. Add ½ cup reserved fat, remove pan from heat, add flour, stir until combined. Return pan to heat, stir until flour is dark golden brown; do not allow to burn. Add water, wine, port, grand marnier, brandy and orange juice, stir until sauce boils and thickens. Season with salt and pepper. Add bayleaf and thyme, stir until combined. Put ducks into individual casserole dishes or one large casserole dish. Pour over sauce, cover, bake in moderate oven for 1½ hours or until ducks are tender. Remove ducks from pan, cut in half lengthwise, put on to serving plates, pour sauce over. Meanwhile, heat mangoes in their own liquid, drain, serve with ducks. Serves 4.

Duck with mangoes.

STUFFING FOR TURKEY

4 rashers bacon
2 medium onions
1 clove garlic
90g (3oz) butter
2.5cm (1in) piece green ginger
6 shallots
2 small red peppers

2 sticks celery
250g (8oz) can water chestnuts
salt, pepper
2 cups fresh breadcrumbs
2 eggs

Heat butter in pan, add peeled and chopped onions, crushed garlic, peeled and grated green ginger, seeded and chopped red peppers, chopped celery and chopped bacon, saute gently until onion is tender, remove pan from heat. Place in bowl breadcrumbs, salt, pepper, chopped shallots, drained and roughly chopped chestnuts, eggs and bacon mixture with fat from pan; mix well. Sufficient for 3kg (6lb) turkey.

Rice & Pasta

Rice makes a change from vegetables with a meal or it can be used an as additional accompaniment. Here are some favourite ways with rice, plus some great sauces for spaghetti

GARLIC RICE
1 cup rice
2 cloves garlic
1 beef stock cube
30g (1oz) butter
3 cups water
2 tablespoons chopped parsley

Melt butter in pan, add crushed garlic, crumbled stock cube and rice, stir over low heat for 5 minutes, add 1 cup water, simmer gently 3 minutes, add remaining water; simmer, uncovered, for further 7 minutes or until rice is tender; drain. Stir in chopped parsley. Serves 4.

BUTTERED WINE-RICE
90g (3oz) butter
1 medium onion
1 cup rice
2½ cups hot water
½ cup dry white wine
4 chicken stock cubes
salt, pepper

Heat butter in frying pan, add peeled and finely chopped onion. Saute gently until onion is tender and light golden brown. Add rice, stir for 3 minutes. Dissolve stock cubes in hot water. Add 1 cup of chicken stock to pan, stir until nearly all liquid is absorbed. Add remaining stock and wine, bring to boil, reduce heat, simmer gently, covered, 10 minutes or until rice is tender. Season with salt and pepper. Serves 4.

RISOTTO MILANESE
375g (12oz) long-grain rice
60g (2oz) butter
1 large onion
½ cup dry white wine
3 cups hot water
2 chicken stock cubes
¼ teaspoon saffron
salt, pepper
30g (1oz) butter, extra

Heat butter in pan, add peeled and finely chopped onion. Saute until onion is tender. Add rice to pan, stir until well coated with butter mixture. Add wine, water, saffron and crumbled stock cubes, bring to boil. Stir well, cover, reduce heat and simmer gently 15 minutes or until all liquid is absorbed and rice is tender. Stir in extra butter, season with salt, pepper. Serves 6.

TOMATO SAUCE FOR SPAGHETTI
30g (1oz) butter
1 tablespoon oil
1 clove garlic
2 medium onions
salt, pepper
2 x 470g (15oz) cans whole tomatoes
2 ripe tomatoes
1 teaspoon sugar
¼ teaspoon oregano
¼ teaspoon basil

Heat butter and oil in pan, add peeled and chopped onions and crushed garlic, saute gently until onions are tender but not brown. Add salt, pepper, undrained canned tomatoes, peeled and chopped ripe tomatoes, sugar, oregano and basil. Bring to boil, stirring; reduce heat, simmer covered for 45 minutes, stirring occasionally. Remove cover, cook until sauce thickens slightly. Serve over hot spaghetti. Serves 4.

SPAGHETTI BOLOGNESE
2 tablespoons oil
2 medium onions
750g (1½lb) minced steak
470g (15oz) can whole tomatoes
3 tablespoons tomato paste
1 teaspoon basil
1 teaspoon oregano
½ teaspoon thyme
salt, pepper
1.25 litres (5 cups) water
grated parmesan cheese

Heat oil in large saucepan, add peeled and chopped onions, saute gently until onions are tender. Add minced steak, stir over high heat until meat is dark golden brown, mashing meat well. Add undrained tomatoes, tomato paste, basil, oregano and thyme; mix well. Season with salt and pepper. Add water; mix well. Bring to boil, reduce heat, simmer uncovered 2 hours or until nearly all liquid has evaporated. Serve over hot spaghetti. Serve with grated parmesan cheese. Serves 4 to 6.

Paella.

Rice & Pasta

SPAGHETTI VONGOLE

2 tablespoons oil
1 small clove garlic
315g (10oz) can baby clams
¼ teaspoon oregano
½ teaspoon basil
4 ripe tomatoes
2 tablespoons chopped parsley
salt, pepper

Heat oil in pan, add crushed garlic and drained clams, saute 1 minute. Add oregano and basil, stir until combined. Add peeled, chopped tomatoes, bring to boil, reduce heat, simmer, uncovered, 15 minutes or until sauce is thick. Add parsley, season with salt and pepper. Serve over hot spaghetti. Serves 4.

BASIL SAUCE FOR SPAGHETTI

90g (3oz) butter
315g (10oz) pkt spinach-in-butter-sauce
1 teaspoon basil
¼ cup dry white wine
1 small onion
¼ cup water
salt, pepper
1 chicken stock cube
1 teaspoon lemon juice
250g (8oz) spaghetti

Heat butter in pan. Add peeled and finely chopped onion. Saute gently until onion is tender. Add spinach, basil, wine, water, salt, pepper and crumbled stock cube. Bring to boil, reduce heat. Simmer, covered, 15 minutes, stirring occasionally. Add lemon juice, stir until combined. Put spaghetti into large pan of boiling salted water. Boil, uncovered, 15 to 20 minutes or until spaghetti is tender; drain. Put spaghetti on serving plates, spoon over hot sauce, top with grated parmesan cheese. Serves 3 to 4.

MEXICAN SPAGHETTI

2 tablespoons oil
1 clove garlic
2 onions
1 green pepper
500g (1lb) minced steak
1 teaspoon chilli powder
1 teaspoon basil
salt, pepper
470g (15oz) can whole tomatoes
½ cup dry red wine
1 beef stock cube
⅓ cup tomato paste

30g (1oz) butter
315g (10oz) can red kidney beans
2 tablespoons chopped parsley
375g (12oz) spaghetti

Heat oil in large pan, add crushed garlic, peeled and finely chopped onions and chopped green pepper, saute until onion is transparent. Add meat to pan, brown well. Stir in chilli powder, basil, salt and pepper; cook, stirring, 1 minute. Add tomatoes with liquid from can, red wine, crumbled stock cube and tomato paste, mix to combine. Cover, reduce heat, simmer 1½ hours, adding a little water if mixture becomes too dry. Cook spaghetti in large pan of boiling salted water until tender, 15 to 20 minutes; drain well; arrange on serving plates. Heat butter in pan, saute drained and rinsed kidney beans for 1 minute, stir in parsley. Spoon meat sauce over top of spaghetti, spoon bean mixture over. Serves 4.

TOMATO CLAM SAUCE

2 tablespoons oil
1 clove garlic
4 ripe tomatoes
½ green pepper
½ teaspoon sugar
½ cup dry white wine
315g (10oz) can baby clams
1 tablespoon chopped parsley

Drain clams, reserve liquid. Heat oil in pan, add crushed garlic and seeded, finely chopped pepper. Saute gently 2 minutes. Add peeled and finely chopped tomatoes, sugar and white wine, stir until combined. Add ½ cup reserved clam liquid; mix well. Bring to boil, stirring, reduce heat; simmer, uncovered, 10 minutes or until sauce is thick. Add clams and parsley, simmer 2 minutes. Season with salt and pepper. Serve over hot spaghetti. Serves 4.

RICH MEAT SAUCE

2 tablespoons oil
30g (1oz) butter
500g (1lb) minced steak
1 large onion
250g (8oz) mushrooms
1 tablespoon flour
1 cup dry red wine
1½ cups water

Greek spaghetti casserole.

1 beef stock cube
2 tablespoons tomato sauce
salt, pepper
½ teaspoon basil

Heat oil and butter in large pan, add meat, mash well. Stir meat until dark golden brown; add peeled and chopped onion and sliced mushrooms, saute 5 minutes. Add flour, stir until combined, remove pan from heat. Add wine, water and crumbled stock cube, stir until combined. Return pan to heat, stir until sauce boils and thickens. Add tomato sauce, salt, pepper and basil; mix well. Reduce heat, simmer, covered, 1 hour or until sauce is thick. Serve over hot spaghetti. Serves 4.

SPAGHETTI ALLA CARBONARA

500g (1lb) spaghetti
boiling salted water
250g (8oz) bacon
½ cup dry white wine
3 eggs
¼ cup cream
½ cup grated parmesan cheese
pepper
chopped parsley
extra grated parmesan cheese

Cook spaghetti in large quantity of boiling salted water for 15 to 20 minutes or until tender but still firm. While spaghetti is cooking, remove rind from

Tomato sauce for spaghetti.

bacon, cut bacon in 1cm (½in) squares. Saute in pan until cooked through but not crisp. Add wine, simmer gently 3 minutes. Drain spaghetti well, return to saucepan. Immediately add bacon and wine. Blend together, then add combined beaten eggs, cream and cheese. Toss together over low heat. Add a little pepper. Make sure spaghetti is coated with egg-and-cheese mixture. Sprinkle with parsley. Serve with extra parmesan cheese. Serves 6 to 8.

PAELLA

60g (2oz) butter
2 tablespoons oil
2 medium onions
1 red pepper
1 green pepper
2 chicken breasts
125g (4oz) bacon pieces
315g (10oz) can artichoke hearts
185g (6oz) frozen peas
500g (1lb) long-grain rice
4½ cups water
2 chicken stock cubes
2 cloves garlic
2 tablespoons chopped parsley
salt, pepper
1 teaspoon saffron
1kg (2lb) mussels
190g (6¾oz) can button mushrooms
500g (1lb) prawns

Heat butter and oil in large pan, gently saute peeled and sliced onions and sliced peppers. Remove meat from chicken breasts, slice meat into 5cm (2in) pieces; thinly slice bacon pieces. Add to pan, brown lightly. Add drained, halved artichoke hearts, peas, rice, water, crumbled stock cubes, crushed garlic, parsley, salt, pepper and saffron. Cover, simmer gently 15 minutes. Scrub mussels well under cold running water, add to pan; cover, cook further 5 to 8 minutes. Remove lid, add drained mushrooms and shelled prawns, stir through well. Check at this stage if rice is cooked and all liquid has evaporated. If rice needs further cooking, add an extra ½ cup hot water. Re-cover, cook further 2 to 3 minutes to heat prawns through. Serves 6.

GREEK SPAGHETTI CASSEROLE

60g (2oz) butter
500g (1lb) minced steak
2 large onions
155g (5oz) can tomato paste
2 cups water
pinch mixed herbs
salt, pepper
375g (12oz) spaghetti
60g (2oz) grated parmesan cheese
2 eggs

½ cup plain flour
3 cups milk
60g (2oz) butter, extra
¼ teaspoon nutmeg

Heat butter in pan, add meat and peeled and finely chopped onions, cook quickly until meat is dark golden brown, mashing meat well. Add tomato paste, water, mixed herbs, salt and pepper, stir until combined. Bring to boil, reduce heat, simmer covered for 45 minutes or until meat is very tender. Gradually add spaghetti to large quantity of boiling salted water, boil uncovered for 15 minutes or until spaghetti is tender; drain. Place spaghetti in bowl, add extra butter, toss spaghetti until butter is melted. Place half the spaghetti in large, well-greased ovenproof dish, sprinkle over half the parmesan cheese. Spoon meat mixture over top, cover with remaining spaghetti. Place sifted flour and eggs in saucepan, stir until flour is free of lumps, gradually add milk, mix until combined. Stir over low heat, until sauce comes to boil, season with salt and pepper. Add nutmeg. Reduce heat, simmer uncovered for 3 minutes. Pour sauce over spaghetti, sprinkle with remaining parmesan cheese. Bake in moderate oven for 40 minutes or until golden brown on top and heated through. Serves 6 to 8.

Vegetables

It is difficult sometimes to think of new ways of cooking and presenting vegetables. You'll like these ideas which add interest to your daily diet

RATATOUILLE
1 large eggplant
3 red peppers
3 green peppers
3 zucchini
2 onions
3 cloves garlic
¾ cup oil
½ teaspoon thyme
1kg (2lb) tomatoes
salt, pepper

Peel eggplant, cut into 2.5cm (1in) cubes. Remove seeds from peppers, cut peppers into 2.5cm (1in) cubes; slice zucchini into rounds; peel and chop onions. Heat 2 tablespoons of the oil in large pan, add onions, crushed garlic and thyme. Cook until onions are transparent; remove from pan. Saute each of the vegetables separately in pan in the remaining oil; add to the onion. Peel tomatoes, chop roughly, add to the other vegetables. Put all the vegetables in a large pan, season with salt and pepper, bring to the boil, reduce heat, simmer uncovered 10 to 15 minutes. Serves 6.

POTATO CASSEROLE
500g (1lb) potatoes
3 onions
30g (1oz) butter
salt, pepper
470g (15oz) can whole tomatoes
1 teaspoon basil
2 cups fresh breadcrumbs
60g (2oz) butter, extra
3 tablespoons grated parmesan cheese
chopped parsley

Peel potatoes, leave whole, cook in boiling salted water until tender; drain, cut into 5mm (¼in) slices. Melt butter in pan, saute peeled and thinly sliced onions until transparent. Arrange half the potatoes in base of ovenproof dish, top with half the onions, season with

salt and pepper. Put tomatoes with liquid from can into bowl, mash with fork, mix in basil. Pour half tomato mixture over potatoes and onions; sprinkle with chopped parsley; repeat with remaining potatoes and onions, pour over remaining tomato mixture, sprinkle with chopped parsley. Melt extra butter in pan, remove from heat, stir in breadcrumbs and cheese, mix well. Sprinkle breadcrumbs over top of dish, bake uncovered in moderate oven 30 to 35 minutes, or until top is golden brown. Serves 4.

CHINESE BROCCOLI
750g (1½lb) fresh broccoli or 2 x 250g (8oz) pkts frozen broccoli
½ cup canned sliced water chestnuts
3 tablespoons oil
1cm (½in) piece green ginger
¼ teaspoon grated lemon rind
½ teaspoon soy sauce
1 tablespoon dry sherry
½ cup water
1 chicken stock cube

Remove stems and leaves from fresh broccoli. If using frozen broccoli, defrost and cut into small flowerets. Put oil, water chestnuts, peeled and grated green ginger and lemon rind into frying pan, simmer until ginger is sizzling. Add broccoli, toss gently in hot oil for 1 minute. Add soy sauce, sherry, water and crumbled stock cube. Bring to boil, reduce heat, simmer covered for 5 minutes or until broccoli is just crisp. Remove vegetables from pan, put on to serving plate. Increase heat, boil remaining liquid in pan until reduced by half, spoon over broccoli. Serves 6.

CAULIFLOWER CHEESE
1 small cauliflower (or quick-frozen cauliflower)

60g (2oz) butter
4 shallots or spring onions
½ cup mayonnaise
salt, pepper
60g (2oz) cheddar cheese
paprika

Separate cauliflower into flowerets; cook in lightly salted water until tender but still firm; drain. Melt butter, saute the chopped shallots or onions for a few moments. Spread shallots or onions and butter over base of shallow ovenproof dish. Cover with the cauliflower, sprinkle lightly with salt and pepper; spread mayonnaise over cauliflower, then sprinkle over the coarsely grated cheese; sprinkle with paprika. Bake in moderate oven approximately 15 minutes, or place under heated griller until cheese is puffed and golden. Serves 4.

CONTINENTAL POTATO CAKES
500g (1lb) potatoes
1 egg
1 tablespoon flour
½ teaspoon salt
oil for frying

Peel potatoes, chop roughly, put in blender, blend on high speed until smooth. Add egg, flour and salt. Blend for further one minute. Pour enough oil in frying pan to cover base, drop tablespoonfuls of mixture into hot oil, fry gently 6 minutes or until golden brown, turning once. Drain on absorbent paper. Sprinkle with salt. Makes approximately 25.

TOMATO-ANCHOVY MUSHROOMS
500g (1lb) medium-sized mushrooms
2 cups fresh white breadcrumbs
3 tablespoons tomato paste

Ratatouille.

1 medium onion
90g (3oz) butter
125g (4oz) cheddar cheese
2 tablespoons chopped parsley
1 egg
salt, pepper
¼ teaspoon oregano
50g (1¾oz) can anchovy fillets

flour
oil for deep-frying

Remove stems from mushrooms, chop stems finely. Heat butter in pan, add peeled and finely chopped onion and mushroom stems, saute until onion is tender. Add tomato paste, stir until combined. Put breadcrumbs in bowl, add tomato paste mixture, grated cheddar cheese, parsley, egg, salt, pepper, oregano and drained and finely chopped anchovy fillets; mix well. Spoon this mixture into mushroom cavities, packing in well. Coat mushrooms with flour, dip in prepared batter, then lower into hot oil; fry until golden brown and cooked through, approximately 3 minutes. Delicious with drinks or as an hors-d'oeuvre.

Batter: Sift into bowl 1½ cups self-raising flour and ½ teaspoon salt, make well in centre, gradually add 1⅓ cups water, mix to smooth batter.

STUFFED PEPPERS
3 medium green peppers
3 medium red peppers
30g (1oz) butter
1 onion
1 clove garlic
750g (1½lb) minced steak
155g (5oz) can tomato paste
1½ cups water
2 beef stock cubes
salt, pepper
½ teaspoon oregano
½ cup dry red wine
30g (1oz) grated parmesan cheese
CHEESE SAUCE
60g (2oz) butter
3 tablespoons flour
1¾ cups milk
pinch nutmeg
salt, pepper
60g (2oz) cheddar cheese
2 eggs, separated

Halve peppers lengthwise, remove seeds. Put peppers into large pan of simmering water, simmer uncovered 2 minutes; drain. Heat butter in large frying pan. Add peeled and chopped onion and meat. Stir until meat is well browned, mashing meat well. Add crushed garlic, tomato paste, water, crumbled stock cubes, salt, pepper, oregano and wine. Stir until mixture comes to boil. Reduce heat, simmer, covered, 60 minutes or until mixture is thick; cool. Carefully spoon meat mixture into pepper halves, then spoon over prepared Cheese Sauce; top each with parmesan cheese. Put on oven tray. Bake in hot oven 10 minutes or until golden brown on top.

Cheese Sauce: Heat butter in pan, add flour, stir until combined. Remove pan from heat, gradually add milk, stir until combined. Return pan to heat, stir until sauce boils and thickens. Add nutmeg, season with salt and pepper. Add grated cheddar cheese, stir until combined. Remove pan from heat, allow to cool slightly. Add egg yolks;

mix well. Return pan to heat, stir until sauce comes to boil, remove from heat. Let sauce cool until warm, then fold in lightly beaten egg whites. Serves 6.

GREEN BEANS ITALIAN
500g (1lb) beans
2 medium onions
¼ cup oil
2 cloves garlic
TOPPING
1 cup fresh breadcrumbs
30g (1oz) butter
2 tablespoons grated parmesan cheese

Top, tail and string beans. Peel and slice onions. Put beans and onions into saucepan. Add enough boiling water to cover beans. Cover, bring to boil again, reduce heat, simmer uncovered 5 minutes; drain. Heat oil in frying pan, add crushed garlic, saute 1 minute. Add beans and onions, saute for 2 minutes. Put on to serving plate, sprinkle with topping.

Topping: Melt butter in pan, add breadcrumbs, stir until golden brown. Remove from pan, allow to cool, then add parmesan cheese; stir until combined. Serves 4.

BRAISED CELERY
8 sticks celery
60g (2oz) butter
1 clove garlic
3 tablespoons water
1 chicken stock cube
salt, pepper

String celery, cut into thin diagonal slices. Heat butter in large pan, add crushed garlic and celery, toss in butter mixture for 3 minutes. Add crumbled stock cube and water, bring to boil, reduce heat, simmer covered 3 minutes. Remove lid, evaporate off any liquid over high heat. Season with salt and pepper. Serves 4.

SPINACH PANCAKES
PANCAKES
1 cup plain flour
¼ teaspoon salt
2 eggs
1 cup milk
FILLING
1 small bunch spinach

salt, pepper
1 teaspoon grated lemon rind
250g (8oz) carton cottage cheese
90g (3oz) cheddar cheese
pinch nutmeg
60g (2oz) butter
1 egg
¼ cup milk
packaged dry breadcrumbs

Pancakes: Sift flour and salt into bowl, add eggs, mix well. Gradually add milk, mix to smooth batter. From small jug pour 2 to 3 tablespoons of batter on greased pan, cook until golden brown; cook on one side only. You will need 6 pancakes.

Filling: Chop spinach into large pieces, remove white stalks. Wash spinach; put in pan with the water that clings to the leaves. Cover, bring to boil, reduce heat, simmer 5 minutes; drain well. Put spinach in bowl, add lemon rind, cottage cheese, grated cheddar cheese and nutmeg; mix well. Season with salt and pepper. Divide spinach mixture evenly on to cooked side of each pancake. Fold into envelope shape, brushing edges with remaining pancake batter. Dip pancakes into combined beaten egg and milk, then into dry breadcrumbs, coating all sides well. Heat butter in pan, add pancakes, cook on both sides until golden brown. Serves 3 or 6.

BAKED CREAMED POTATOES
1kg (2lb) old potatoes
1 cup mayonnaise
½ cup sour cream
¼ cup milk
2 eggs
2 teaspoons prepared mustard
salt, pepper
2 tablespoons chopped parsley
90g (3oz) cheese
¼ cup grated parmesan cheese

Peel and chop potatoes, cook in boiling salted water until tender, drain well. Mash until smooth, mix with mayonnaise, sour cream, milk, lightly beaten eggs, mustard and parsley; season with salt and pepper. Press mixture through sieve, spoon mixture evenly into greased ovenproof dish. Sprinkle with combined grated cheeses. Bake in moderate oven 20 to 30 minutes or until golden on top. Serves 4 to 6.

Continental potato cakes.

Chinese Vegetables

VEGETABLES cooked in the Chinese manner are crisp and colourful. Hot oil seals in the vegetable juices and colour; water is added, the pan covered and the vegetables steam until tender yet remain delightfully crisp. Because cooking time is so short, they are full of flavour and nourishment and can be enjoyed on their own as a complete meal or as an extra dish with other food.

YOU WILL NEED:
¼ cup oil
1 tablespoon finely chopped green ginger
3 onions
375g (12oz) carrots
½ medium cauliflower
1 cup water
2 chicken stock cubes
500g (1lb) beans
6 sticks celery
1 red pepper
1 green pepper
250g (8oz) zucchini
½ medium cabbage
10 shallots

Step 1: Prepare vegetables as shown above. Peel and quarter onions; scrape carrots, slice finely; break cauliflower into flowerets; string beans and celery, slice diagonally; cut peppers into 2.5cm (1in) cubes; slice zucchini finely; shred cabbage finely; chop half the shallots finely, slice remainder finely and reserve for garnishing.

Step 2: Heat oil in wok or large frying pan. Add ginger, onions, carrots and cauliflower; stir gently to coat all vegetables with oil. Add water and crumbled stock cubes, bring to boil, cover, boil 3 minutes.

Step 3: Remove lid, add beans, celery, peppers, zucchini and chopped shallots; cover; cook until vegetables are just tender (approximately 5 minutes). Remove lid to stir occasionally.

Step 4: Remove lid, scatter cabbage over top of vegetables; cover again, cook further 2 to 3 minutes. Remove lid, stir cabbage gently through other vegetables. Garnish with sliced shallots. Quantities given serve four as a main meal or eight as an accompaniment.

Chinese vegetables.

Vegetarian Dishes

Vegetarians and non-vegetarians alike will find these recipes offer new, nutritious food ideas for the family

VEGETABLE PASTIES
PASTRY
2 cups wholemeal plain flour
½ teaspoon vegetable salt
60g (2oz) vegetable margarine
½ cup water
oil for deep-frying
FILLING
60g (2oz) vegetable margarine
1 large onion
1 clove garlic
500g (1lb) ripe tomatoes
2 sticks celery
1 red pepper
470g (15oz) can red kidney beans
vegetable salt

Pastry: Sift flour and salt into bowl, rub in margarine until mixture resembles fine breadcrumbs. Add water, mix to a pliable dough. Turn out on to lightly floured surface, knead 5 minutes. Cover pastry, stand 1 hour, knead again 3 minutes. Roll out to 3mm (⅛in) thickness. Cut into rounds, using 15cm (6in) round cutter, or use saucer as guide. Brush edges with a little water, spoon 2 tablespoons filling into centre of each round. Pinch edges together, put into deep hot oil, fry until golden brown, approximately 2 minutes.

Filling: Heat margarine in pan, add peeled and chopped onion and crushed garlic, saute until onion is tender. Add roughly chopped tomatoes, chopped celery, seeded and chopped pepper, drained and rinsed beans and vegetable salt, stir until combined. Cover, simmer gently 15 minutes, remove lid, simmer further 10 minutes or until mixture is thick. Allow to cool. Makes 8 pasties.

SPINACH PIE
PASTRY
1½ cups wholemeal plain flour
1 teaspoon vegetable salt
1½ cups wheatgerm
125g (4oz) vegetable margarine
⅓ cup water, approximately
FILLING
2 bunches spinach (approximately 20 stalks)
500g (1lb) potatoes
250g (8oz) cottage cheese
½ teaspoon basil
¼ teaspoon mixed herbs
¼ teaspoon nutmeg
1 teaspoon vegetable salt

Pastry: Sift flour and salt into bowl, add husks in sifter to flour, fold in wheatgerm. Rub in margarine until mixture resembles coarse breadcrumbs, mix with enough water to make a stiff dough; knead lightly. Roll out half pastry on floured surface to 23cm (9in) circle, using saucepan lid as guide. Put pastry circle on to greased oven tray, spoon over cold spinach mixture, spreading to within 2.5cm (1in) of edge of circle, piling up in the centre. Brush edge of pastry with water. Roll out remaining pastry to 30cm (12in) circle. Carefully lift over spinach, easing edges together; press edges together with fork. Trim edge with sharp knife, make two slits in top of pastry. Brush pastry with water. Bake in hot oven 15 minutes, reduce heat to moderate, cook further 15 to 20 minutes or until golden brown.

Filling: Wash and chop spinach. Put in saucepan with just enough water to cover base of saucepan, cover, cook until tender, drain well. Peel potatoes, cut into cubes, cook in salted water until tender; drain. Combine spinach, potato, cottage cheese, basil, mixed herbs, nutmeg and salt, mix well, allow to cool. Serves 4 to 6.

SESAME STICKS
250g (8oz) fresh or canned bean curd
1 egg
1 tablespoon cornflour
1 teaspoon vegetable salt
¼ teaspoon five spice powder
1 teaspoon sesame oil
12 slices wholemeal bread
sesame seeds
oil for deep-frying

Drain bean curd, combine with beaten egg, cornflour, salt, five spice powder and sesame oil, mix well. Remove crusts from bread, spread paste over bread, sprinkle with sesame seeds.

Spinach pie.

Vegetarian Dishes

Cut each slice into 3 even sticks. Deep-fry in hot oil until golden brown. Serve as a party savoury.

HERBED VEGETABLE FLAN
PASTRY
1 cup wholemeal plain flour
1 teaspoon vegetable salt
1 cup wheatgerm
60g (2oz) vegetable margarine
¼ cup water
FILLING
1 tablespoon oil
2 tablespoons wholemeal flour
410g (13oz) can vegetable juice
2 zucchini
2 medium carrots
1 onion
1 clove garlic
¼ teaspoon mixed herbs
60g (2oz) mushrooms
TOPPING
1 cup wholemeal breadcrumbs
1 tablespoon oil
1 clove garlic
1 tablespoon chopped parsley

Pastry: Sift flour and salt into bowl, add wheatgerm, mix well. Rub in margarine until mixture resembles fine breadcrumbs. Gradually add water, mix to a firm dough. Roll out pastry on lightly floured surface to line 23cm (9in) flan tin. Prick base of flan with fork, bake in moderate oven 12 to 15 minutes or until pastry is cooked; cool.

Filling: Heat oil in pan, add flour, blend until smooth, gradually stir in vegetable juice. Bring mixture to boil, stirring constantly. Add finely sliced zucchini, peeled and finely grated carrots, peeled and thinly sliced onion, crushed garlic and mixed herbs. Reduce heat, simmer over low heat until vegetables are tender. Roughly chop mushrooms, add to pan, cook further 2 minutes; cool. Spoon mixture evenly into flan case, sprinkle over bread-crumb topping, bake uncovered in moderate oven 10 to 15 minutes.

Topping: Heat oil in pan, add crushed garlic and breadcrumbs, stir until crumbs are golden brown. Remove from heat, add parsley, mix well. Serves 4 to 6.

VEGETARIAN SPAGHETTI
1 tablespoon oil
1 large onion
1 clove garlic
500g (1lb) tomatoes
½ teaspoon mixed herbs
1 cup water
salt
250g (8oz) wholemeal spaghetti
470g (15oz) can nutmeat

Cook spaghetti in boiling salted water 12 to 15 minutes or until tender; drain. Heat oil in pan, add peeled and finely chopped onion and crushed garlic, saute until onion is transparent. Add nutmeat, mix well, cook 1 minute. Stir in peeled and roughly chopped tomatoes, mixed herbs and water, mix well. Season with salt, cover, simmer gently 10 minutes; add extra ½ cup of water if mixture becomes too dry. Serve over spaghetti. Serves 4.

HOT RICE SALAD WITH VEGETABLES
1 cup brown rice
¼ cup oil
375g (12oz) packet frozen broccoli
1 red pepper
3 sticks celery
6 shallots
6 radishes
vegetable salt
1 teaspoon soy sauce

Gradually add rice to large quantity of boiling salted water, boil uncovered for 20 to 25 minutes or until rice is tender; drain. Defrost broccoli, cut into sections. Heat oil in frying pan, add broccoli, seeded and cubed red pepper, sliced celery, chopped shallots and sliced radishes, cook quickly for 3 minutes. Add rice, toss for 3 minutes. Season with salt. Add soy sauce just before serving, toss until combined. Or rice, with the soy sauce added, can be placed in serving dish and the vegetables arranged on top. Serves 6.

COTTAGE CHEESE LOAF
1kg (2lb) cottage cheese
2 cups rolled oats
2 large onions

Sesame sticks.

3 eggs
vegetable salt
2 teaspoons mixed herbs
⅓ cup milk

Peel and grate onions or chop very finely. Combine all ingredients, blend together well. One tablespoon of soy sauce also can be blended in. Pour into well-greased, deep 20cm (8in) casserole. Bake in moderate oven approximately 1 hour or until firm. Serves 6.

APRICOT HEALTH DRINK
2 tablespoons cottage cheese
3 tablespoons plain yoghurt
2 teaspoons honey
185g (6oz) can apricot nectar
6 ice-cubes

Put cottage cheese, honey and yoghurt in blender, blend on medium speed until smooth. Gradually add apricot nectar, blend until combined. Add ice-cubes, blend further 1 minute. Serves 2.

ORANGE HEALTH DRINK
⅓ cup orange juice
1 tablespoon lemon juice
1 tablespoon wheatgerm
1 tablespoon honey
1 egg

Combine all ingredients in blender, blend until frothy. Serves 1.

Hot rice salad with vegetables.

Salads

Cool, crisp and colourful or hot and hearty — a range of salads to add interest and flavour to any meal

CURRIED EGG SALAD
8 eggs
2 sticks celery
4 shallots
3 tablespoons chopped parsley
6 thin slices square white bread
60g (2oz) butter
3 tablespoons grated parmesan cheese
lettuce leaves
CURRY MAYONNAISE
1 medium onion
60g (2oz) butter
1 tablespoon curry powder
½ cup mayonnaise
1 tablespoon lemon juice
½ cup cream
salt, pepper

Put eggs into saucepan of cold water, cover, bring to boil, reduce heat, simmer 8 to 10 minutes. Drain, put into cold water. Shell eggs when cold. Put thinly sliced celery, chopped shallots and parsley into bowl, mix well. Remove crusts from bread, cut each slice into 3 rounds using 4cm (1½in) cutter. Put rounds on to oven tray, brush each side with melted butter; sprinkle over parmesan cheese. Bake in moderate oven 10 minutes or until golden brown; cool. Line serving plate with lettuce leaves. Put halved eggs on one side of plate, spoon celery mixture beside eggs, then put bread rounds next to celery mixture. Refrigerate until ready to serve. Offer Curry Mayonnaise separately.

Curry Mayonnaise: Heat butter in pan, add peeled and finely chopped onion, saute gently until onion is transparent; add curry powder, cook 1 minute; allow to become cold. Combine onion and butter mixture with mayonnaise, lemon juice, salt and pepper. Beat cream until soft peaks form, fold into mayonnaise mixture. Serves 6 to 8.

HOT VEGETABLE SALAD
125g (4oz) green beans
125g (4oz) button mushrooms
6 small onions
½ green pepper
½ red pepper
2 tomatoes
2 sticks celery
¼ cup oil
DRESSING
½ cup french dressing
¼ cup oil
1 teaspoon curry powder
2 teaspoons sugar
salt, pepper

Trim and string beans, cut into 5cm (2in) lengths; trim mushrooms; peel and quarter onions; remove stalks from peppers, cut into strips; cut tomatoes into quarters; cut celery diagonally into 2.5cm (1in) slices. Saute vegetables in hot oil 4 minutes, put into large salad bowl. Add dressing and toss lightly.

Dressing: Combine all ingredients in screw-top jar, shake well. Serves 4 to 6.

ITALIAN MIXED SALAD
125g (4oz) green beans
125g (4oz) button mushrooms
12 small onions
1 green pepper
2 carrots
1 small cauliflower
1 small eggplant
2 sticks celery
¼ cup oil
DRESSING
½ cup bottled italian dressing
¼ cup oil
1 clove garlic
2 teaspoons prepared mustard
2 teaspoons sugar

Trim and string beans, cut into 5cm (2in) lengths; trim mushrooms; peel and quarter onions; remove stalk from pepper, cut into strips; peel carrots, cut diagonally into 2.5cm (1in) chunks; divide cauliflower into flowerets; cut unpeeled eggplant into 2.5cm (1in) cubes; cut celery diagonally into 2.5cm (1in) slices. Saute vegetables in hot oil five minutes, put into large salad bowl. Add dressing and toss lightly.

Dressing: Combine all ingredients in screw-top jar, shake well. Serves 6.

ITALIAN PRAWN SALAD
500g (1lb) prawns
2 tomatoes
470g (15oz) can artichoke hearts
60g (2oz) sliced salami
60g (2oz) black olives
lettuce leaves
DRESSING
½ cup oil
⅓ cup lemon juice
1 teaspoon sugar
1 teaspoon prepared mustard
1 tablespoon chopped parsley

Shell prawns, remove back vein; cut

Curried egg salad.

Mango and orange salad.

Curried seafood salad.

Hot potato salad.

Salads

in half, if large. Remove stems from tomatoes, cut into quarters; drain artichoke hearts, cut in half. Combine prawns, tomato quarters, artichoke pieces, salami and black olives in bowl, toss to combine. Spoon mixture into lettuce leaves. Before serving, spoon dressing over.

Dressing: Combine all ingredients in screw-top jar. Shake well. Serves 4 as an entree or luncheon dish.

GREEK SALAD
1 small red pepper
1 small green pepper
1 large onion
125g (4oz) black olives
2 ripe tomatoes
2 sticks celery
1 cucumber
1 small lettuce
125g (4oz) feta cheese
¼ cup french dressing

Cut red and green peppers into rings, remove any seeds. Peel onion, cut into wedges, separate into pieces. Cut tomatoes into wedges. Cut celery into slices. Cut cucumber into cubes. Wash and dry lettuce, tear into pieces. Put all prepared vegetables into salad bowl, add olives, cover, refrigerate until ready to serve. Add salad dressing, toss well, top salad with sliced feta cheese. Serves 6 to 8.

HOT POTATO SALAD
1kg (2lb) potatoes
2 sticks celery
1 onion
½ red pepper
2 tablespoons chopped parsley
¼ cup sour cream
⅓ cup french dressing
salt, pepper
2 rashers bacon
2 hard-boiled eggs
90g (3oz) cheese

Peel and dice potatoes, cook in boiling salted water until tender; drain well. Slice celery diagonally, peel and finely chop onion, slice red pepper. Combine hot potatoes, celery, onion, pepper and parsley in bowl. Mix sour cream and dressing until smooth, season with salt and pepper, pour over potato mixture, mix lightly, spoon into shallow ovenproof dish. Dice bacon, saute in pan until crisp. Drain, sprinkle over top

of potatoes with chopped eggs. Grate cheese, sprinkle over top of bacon and eggs, heat under hot griller until cheese has melted and is golden brown. Delicious as an accompaniment to steak, chops etc. Serves 6.

CREAMY POTATO COLESLAW
500g (1lb) large potatoes
½ small cabbage
½ red pepper
½ green pepper
1 stick celery
½ cucumber
4 shallots
2 tablespoons chopped parsley
DRESSING
¼ cup sour cream
⅓ cup mayonnaise
¼ cup french dressing
salt, pepper
1 teaspoon french mustard
2 tablespoons finely chopped mint

Peel and dice potatoes, cook until tender; drain, allow to cool. Wash and finely shred cabbage, put into bowl. Add seeded and chopped red and green peppers, sliced celery, peeled and diced cucumber, chopped shallots, potatoes and parsley; toss lightly. Pour over prepared dressing; toss well.

Dressing: Put all ingredients into bowl; mix well. Serves 4 to 6.

MANGO AND ORANGE SALAD
1 lettuce
500g (1lb) can mango slices
3 oranges
3 sticks celery
6 shallots
1 cucumber
CREAM DRESSING
⅓ cup mayonnaise
⅓ cup cream
salt, pepper
2 tablespoons chopped parsley
½ teaspoon grated orange rind
1 teaspoon french mustard

Wash lettuce, gently separate lettuce cups on to large serving plate. Drain mangoes; peel oranges and remove all white pith, cut oranges into segments. To make celery curls, cut celery into 8cm (3in) sticks, slice celery into very thin strips, leaving intact at one end. Put into iced water until celery curls. Score skin of cucumber with fork, cut cucumber into thin slices. Divide

Greek salad.

mangoes, oranges, celery curls and cucumber evenly between lettuce cups. Sprinkle chopped shallots over. Refrigerate until ready to serve. Serve dressing separately.

Cream Dressing: Combine all ingredients in bowl; mix well. Let stand 15 minutes before using. Serves 6 to 8.

Note: This salad is particularly good with cold roast pork or chicken.

CURRIED SEAFOOD SALAD

1½ cups long-grain rice
500g (1lb) prawns
500g (1lb) scallops
60g (2oz) butter
2 sticks celery
2 tablespoons chopped parsley
3 shallots
1 small red pepper
½ cup french dressing
2 teaspoons curry powder
1 teaspoon turmeric
2 teaspoons lemon juice
salt, pepper
¼ teaspoon sugar

Gradually add rice to large quantity of boiling salted water, boil uncovered 12 minutes or until rice is tender; drain. Spread rice out on flat tray and leave 2 hours or until rice is dry. Shell prawns, remove back vein. Heat butter in pan, add scallops, cook gently, stirring, 3 to 5 minutes or until scallops are tender; drain. Place rice in large bowl, add prawns, scallops, finely chopped celery, parsley, chopped shallots, seeded and finely chopped pepper; toss lightly. Combine french dressing, curry powder, turmeric, lemon juice and sugar in bowl, season with salt and pepper. Add dressing to rice mixture; toss thoroughly. Refrigerate until ready to serve. Serves 6.

Sauces

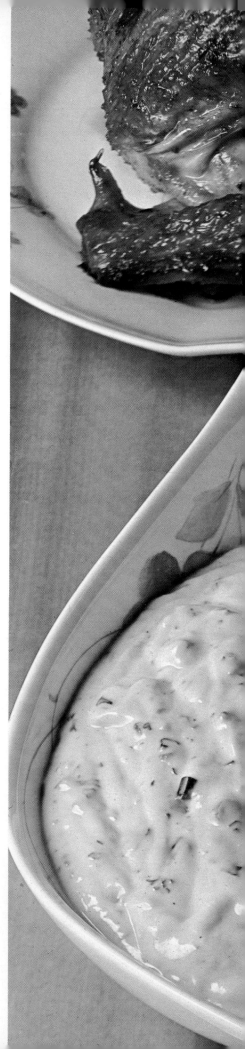

**Roast chicken, fish, steak, chops
or sausages gain interest and flavour
when you spoon over a special sauce**

ONION MADEIRA SAUCE
90g (3oz) butter
2 large onions
1 clove garlic
3 tablespoons flour
2 cups water
470g (15oz) can whole tomatoes
¼ cup madeira or dry sherry
salt, pepper
2 tablespoons chopped parsley
2 beef stock cubes

Heat butter in pan, add peeled and sliced onions and crushed garlic, saute gently until onions are dark golden brown. Add flour, stir until flour is dark golden brown, remove pan from heat. Add water and undrained tomatoes, stir until combined, mashing tomatoes. Return pan to heat, stir until sauce boils and thickens. Add madeira or sherry, salt, pepper and crumbled stock cubes. Reduce heat, cover, simmer sauce 30 minutes, stirring occasionally. Remove pan from heat, push sauce through fine sieve. Return pan to heat, bring to boil, add parsley. Serve with beef or lamb. Serves 6.

WINE-CREAM SAUCE
1 large onion
1 cup water
½ cup dry white wine
2 chicken stock cubes
1 tablespoon cornflour
2 tablespoons water, extra
salt, pepper
½ cup mayonnaise
1 cup sour cream

6 shallots
2 tablespoons chopped parsley
1 teaspoon french mustard
2 teaspoons horseradish relish

Put peeled and chopped onion, water, white wine and crumbled stock cubes into pan. Bring to boil, reduce heat, simmer uncovered until liquid is reduced by half; remove pan from heat. Add combined cornflour and extra water, stir until combined. Return pan to heat, stir until sauce boils and thickens, simmer uncovered 2 minutes. Strain sauce; discard onion. Put sauce into bowl, allow to cool. Add mayonnaise, chopped shallots, parsley, mustard, relish, salt and pepper; mix well. Put sour cream in bowl. Beat until soft peaks form, gently fold into mayonnaise mixture. Cover bowl, refrigerate until ready to serve. Serve with chicken or fish. Serves 6.

MUSTARD SAUCE
30g (1oz) butter
1½ tablespoons flour
1 cup water
1 beef stock cube
3 tablespoons mayonnaise
1 tablespoon prepared mustard
1 teaspoon lemon juice
salt, pepper

Melt butter in pan, stir in flour, cook 1 minute. Gradually stir in water, add crumbled stock cube, mayonnaise, mustard and lemon juice. Simmer 2 minutes, season with salt and pepper. Serve with meat or fish. Serves 4.

Wine-cream sauce and Onion madeira sauce.

Sauces

PORT AND ONION SAUCE

2 large onions
90g (3oz) butter
2 tablespoons flour
salt, pepper
1 cup water
2 beef stock cubes
1 cup dry red wine
1 tablespoon brandy
¼ cup port
1 teaspoon worcestershire sauce
1 tablespoon port, extra

Heat butter in pan, add peeled and thinly sliced onions, saute gently until onions are dark golden brown. Add flour, stir until dark golden brown. Remove pan from heat, add water, crumbled stock cubes, wine, brandy, port and worcestershire sauce, stir until combined. Return pan to heat, stir until sauce boils and thickens. Season with salt and pepper. Cover pan, simmer gently 20 minutes. Just before serving, stir in extra port. Serve with beef or lamb. Serves 4.

AVOCADO BEARNAISE

4 tablespoons white vinegar
2 shallots
1 bayleaf
6 peppercorns
salt, pepper
4 egg yolks
250g (8oz) butter
1 tablespoon lemon juice
1 ripe avocado

Put vinegar, chopped shallots, bayleaf and peppercorns into pan, bring to boil. Reduce heat, simmer very gently uncovered until mixture is reduced by half; strain, cool. Put egg yolks in top of double saucepan, add cold liquid, mix well. Melt butter in pan, cool. Put top of double saucepan over simmering water, gradually add butter, stir constantly until mixture is thick and creamy; remove from heat immediately. Add lemon juice, season with salt and pepper. Put sauce into blender, add peeled and chopped avocado, blend on medium speed until smooth. Put into serving bowl. Serve with beef or fish. Serves 4 to 6.

CURRY-CREAM SAUCE

2 onions
60g (2oz) butter
3 teaspoons curry powder
¾ cup mayonnaise
¼ cup cream
2 teaspoons lemon juice
1 tablespoon chopped parsley
salt

Saute peeled and roughly chopped onions in butter until onions are transparent, add curry powder. Put into blender, blend until of puree consistency. Return to pan with mayonnaise, cream, lemon juice, chopped parsley and salt. Stir over heat until sauce just comes to the boil. Remove from heat immediately. Serve with chicken, fish or meat. Serves 4.

BARBECUE SAUCE

1 onion
125g (4oz) butter
½ cup vinegar
1 cup tomato juice
1 cup tomato sauce
1 tablespoon worcestershire sauce
¼ cup brown sugar
1 teaspoon dry mustard
1 teaspoon salt
1 teaspoon paprika

Melt butter in pan, add finely chopped onion, saute 5 minutes. Add vinegar, tomato juice, tomato sauce, worcestershire sauce, brown sugar, mustard, salt and paprika, bring to boil, reduce heat, simmer for 15 to 20 minutes. Makes approximately 2 cups.

DILL SAUCE

⅔ cup mayonnaise
⅔ cup sour cream
1 teaspoon dried dill (or 1 tablespoon finely chopped fresh dill)
1 small onion
2 tablespoons finely chopped parsley
2 teaspoons lemon juice
¼ teaspoon dry mustard
salt, pepper

Combine grated onion and remaining ingredients in bowl. Mix thoroughly. Serve with fish. Serves 6.

TOMATO SAUCE

2.5kg (5lb) ripe tomatoes
3 green apples
2 cloves garlic
1¾ cups sugar
2 teaspoons salt
¼ teaspoon pepper
6 whole cloves
8 whole allspice
1 teaspoon ground ginger
2 cups white vinegar

Put roughly chopped tomatoes, roughly chopped apples, chopped garlic, sugar, salt, pepper, cloves, allspice, ginger and vinegar into large pan. Bring to boil, reduce heat, simmer covered for 20 minutes or until tomatoes and apples are very tender. Push mixture through sieve. Return to pan, bring to boil, boil uncovered for 25 minutes or until mixture is thick, stirring occasionally. Makes approximately 4 cups.

Avocado bearnaise.

Cakes

If you love cake, then every recipe here will become a favourite

FRUIT LOAF

1 cup currants
1 cup sultanas
1 cup chopped raisins
½ cup chopped dates
¼ cup chopped mixed peel
1 cup brown sugar, lightly packed
1 cup strong tea
1 egg
1 tablespoon brandy
1 cup plain flour
1 cup self-raising flour
60g (2oz) chopped walnuts

Combine fruit, peel, brown sugar and tea in bowl, cover, stand overnight. Add combined beaten egg and brandy, sifted flours and chopped walnuts, mix well. Grease 23cm by 12cm (9in by 5in) loaf tin, line base with greased greaseproof paper. Spread cake mixture evenly into tin. Bake in moderately slow oven 1½ hours or until cooked when tested. Turn out and cool on wire rack. Cut into slices, serve buttered.

GINGER CAKE

1½ cups plain flour
1 cup self-raising flour
1 teaspoon bicarbonate of soda
2 teaspoons ground ginger
½ teaspoon cinnamon
½ teaspoon mixed spice
pinch salt
1 cup sugar
2 eggs
1 cup milk
125g (4oz) butter
1 cup golden syrup

LEMON ICING

1 cup icing sugar
2 teaspoons lemon juice
2 teaspoons butter

Sift flours, soda, ginger, cinnamon, mixed spice and salt into bowl. Add sugar, beaten eggs and milk, mix well. Put butter and golden syrup into saucepan, stir over low heat until butter has melted. Stir into flour mixture, mix until well combined. Grease deep 20cm (8in) square tin, line with greased greaseproof paper. Pour cake mixture evenly into tin. Bake in moderate oven 1 hour to 1¼ hours or until cooked when tested. Leave in tin 10 minutes before turning out on wire rack to cool. When cold, top with Lemon Icing.

Lemon Icing: Sift icing sugar into bowl, add lemon juice and softened butter, mix well.

BEST EVER SPONGE

4 eggs
¾ cup castor sugar
⅔ cup plain flour
⅓ cup cornflour
1 teaspoon baking powder

Beat eggs until thick and creamy, gradually add sugar, beat until sugar has dissolved. Gently fold in sifted dry ingredients. Pour mixture into two greased 20cm (8in) round sandwich tins. Bake in moderate oven 20 to 25 minutes or until cakes shrink slightly from sides of tins. When cold, sandwich with jam and whipped cream. Decorate top with whipped cream and strawberries.

Chestnut-chocolate torte.

Cakes

GREEK COCONUT CAKE
125g (4oz) butter
1 cup sugar
4 eggs
2 cups coconut
1 cup self-raising flour
SYRUP
1½ cups sugar
1¼ cups water
4 thin strips lemon rind

Cream butter and sugar until light and fluffy. Add well-beaten eggs, beat in well. Fold in coconut and sifted flour, mix well. Spread mixture into greased deep 20cm (8in) square cake tin. Bake in hot oven 10 to 15 minutes or until top is golden brown, reduce heat to slow, bake further 25 to 30 minutes or until cooked when tested. Allow to stand 5 minutes in tin, then pour over prepared syrup. Allow cake to become cold in tin before turning out.

Syrup: Place all ingredients in pan, stir over low heat until sugar has dissolved, increase heat, bring to boil, reduce heat, simmer 5 minutes. Remove lemon rind, pour hot syrup over cake.

SULTANA LOAF
125g (4oz) butter
½ cup sugar
2 eggs
1 tablespoon grated orange rind
1 cup sultanas
2 cups self-raising flour
⅔ cup milk

Cream butter and sugar until light and creamy, add eggs one at a time, beating well after each addition, beat in orange rind. Mix in sultanas, add sifted flour alternately with milk, mix well. Grease two 25cm by 8cm (10in by 3in) bar tins, line bases with greased greaseproof paper. Spread mixture evenly in tins, bake in moderate oven 30 to 35 minutes or until cooked when tested. Turn out and cool on wire rack.

Note: This mixture also fits nicely into a 23cm by 12cm (9in by 5in) loaf tin lined, as above, with greased greaseproof paper. For this size tin, bake in moderate oven 45 to 50 minutes. Mixture also may be halved to make one small cake suitable for two.

ORANGE SULTANA CAKE
250g (8oz) butter
1 cup sugar
3 cups self-raising flour
2 tablespoons grated orange rind
½ cup orange juice
4 eggs
1½ cups sultanas

Place all ingredients except sultanas in large bowl of electric mixer, beat on medium speed 2 minutes until mixture is well blended. (Do not over-beat or mixture will be crumbly). Stir in sultanas. Grease deep 20cm (8in) round tin, line base with greased greaseproof paper. Spoon mixture evenly into tin. Bake in moderate oven 1¼ to 1½ hours or until cooked when tested.

BOILED FRUIT CAKE
375g (12oz) packet mixed fruit
½ cup chopped dates
½ cup sultanas
60g (2oz) dried apricots
½ cup apricot jam
½ cup orange juice
250g (8oz) butter
¾ cup brown sugar, lightly packed
2 cups self-raising flour
1 teaspoon mixed spice
1 teaspoon cinnamon
1 teaspoon ground ginger
1 tablespoon brandy
3 eggs

Combine mixed fruit, remaining chopped fruit, jam, orange juice, butter and brown sugar in large saucepan. Stir over low heat until butter melts and sugar has dissolved, increase heat, bring

**Left: Orange sultana cake.
Right: Ginger cake and,
at right, Fruit loaf.**

Cakes

to boil, reduce heat, simmer 5 minutes, let stand until cold. Add combined beaten eggs and brandy, then fold in sifted dry ingredients. Grease deep 20cm (8in) square tin, line with greased greaseproof paper, spread mixture evenly into tin. Bake in moderately slow oven 2 to 2½ hours or until cooked when tested.

ORANGE SOUR CREAM CAKE

90g (3oz) butter
1 tablespoon grated orange rind
¾ cup castor sugar
2 eggs
1½ cups plain flour
½ teaspoon bicarbonate of soda
½ cup sour cream

Line base and sides of 23cm by 12cm (9in by 5in) loaf tin with one layer of greased greaseproof paper, bringing paper 2.5cm (1in) above edge of tin. Beat butter and orange rind until soft and creamy, add sugar, beat until light and fluffy. Add eggs one at a time, beating well after each addition. Stir in sifted flour and soda alternately with sour cream, beat lightly until smooth. Spread evenly into prepared tin, bake in slow oven approximately 1¼ hours or until cooked when tested. Turn on to wire rack to cool. Before slicing, dust top with icing sugar.

CHOCOLATE PEPPERMINT CAKE

125g (4oz) butter
⅔ cup castor sugar
2 eggs
½ teaspoon vanilla
4 tablespoons cocoa
½ cup hot water
1½ cups self-raising flour
PEPPERMINT ICING
1 cup icing sugar
1 teaspoon butter
1 tablespoon milk, approximately
peppermint essence
CHOCOLATE ICING
1 cup icing sugar
1 teaspoon butter
2 tablespoons cocoa
2 tablespoons water, approximately

Cream butter and sugar until soft and creamy. Add vanilla, beat well. Add eggs one at a time, beating well after each addition. Combine cocoa and hot water, stir until smooth and free from lumps. When cold, fold cocoa mixture and sifted flour into creamed mixture, mix to a smooth consistency. Spoon into greased 20cm (8in) ring tin. Bake in moderate oven 40 to 45 minutes or until cooked when tested. When cold, spoon prepared Peppermint Icing on top of cake. When set, spoon Chocolate Icing over Peppermint.

Peppermint Icing: Sift icing sugar into bowl, add butter and enough milk to mix to a thick paste. Stand bowl over pan of simmering water, stir until icing is shiny and smooth. Flavour with a few drops of peppermint essence.

Chocolate Icing: Sift icing sugar and cocoa into bowl, add butter and enough water to mix to thick paste. Stand bowl over pan of simmering water, stir until shiny and smooth.

CHESTNUT-CHOCOLATE TORTE

4 eggs, separated
½ cup castor sugar
½ teaspoon vanilla
1 tablespoon brandy
280g (9oz) can chestnut spread
½ cup self-raising flour
1 cup cream
90g (3oz) dark chocolate
1 cup cream, extra
60g (2oz) dark chocolate, extra

Beat egg yolks, sugar and vanilla together until thick and creamy. Add brandy and ½ cup of the chestnut spread (reserve remainder for filling). Lightly fold in sifted flour, mix thoroughly. Beat egg whites until soft peaks form, gently fold into cake mixture. Grease two 20cm (8in) round sandwich tins, line bases with greased greaseproof paper. Spread cake evenly into prepared tins, bake in moderate oven 20 to 25 minutes or until cooked, turn out of tins, cool. Melt 90g (3oz) chocolate in top of double saucepan over simmering water, cool slightly, spread evenly on flat side of each half of cake. Whip 1 cup cream, fold in remaining chestnut spread. Place one half of cake on to serving plate chocolate-side up; spread chestnut filling evenly over cake, top with the other half of cake, chocolate side down. Spread extra whipped cream over top and sides of cake and decorate top with extra grated chocolate. Refrigerate several hours before cutting.

Sultana loaf.

Best ever sponge.

STRAWBERRY HAZELNUT GATEAU

LAYERS of hazelnut meringue, coated with chocolate and filled with strawberries and cream, combine deliciously in this superb cake for special occasions.

YOU WILL NEED:
4 egg whites
pinch salt
1¼ cups castor sugar
90g (3oz) ground hazelnuts
1 teaspoon vinegar
½ teaspoon vanilla
185g (6oz) dark chocolate
¼ cup water
1 cup cream
1 punnet strawberries
1½ cups cream, extra

Step 1: Beat egg whites with salt until soft peaks form, gradually add sugar; beat until sugar is dissolved and mixture is of meringue consistency. Beat in vinegar and vanilla. Line bases and sides of two 20cm (8in) springform pans with greased greaseproof paper which has been lightly dusted with cornflour. Spread meringue mixture evenly into tins. Sprinkle ground hazelnuts evenly over meringue in both tins. With knife or small spatula, swirl hazelnuts lightly through meringue. Smooth over top of meringue with back of spoon. Bake in moderate oven 35 to 40 minutes or until meringue is crisp to touch; release sides of pan, cool on base of pan.

Step 2: Chop chocolate. Combine with water in top of double saucepan; stir over simmering water until melted; cool. Remove cakes from bases. Place a layer of meringue on serving plate, flat side down; spread with a thin layer of chocolate. Spread whipped cream over chocolate. Reserve 4 strawberries, wash and hull remainder, cut in half, arrange over cream. Spread underside of second layer of meringue with remaining chocolate mixture, place on top of strawberry layer, chocolate-side down. Whip extra cream, cover sides and top of cake and, if desired, pipe cream decoratively on top. Arrange reserved halved strawberries on top of cake. Refrigerate until ready to use. If desired, brush strawberries used for decoration with warmed, sieved strawberry jam to give them a pretty glaze before arranging on cake.

Cake of "Kisses"

THIS cake of tiny meringue "kisses" makes a spectacular dessert or birthday cake. Meringue layers and individual meringues can be made a day or two beforehand (store them in an air-tight container) and assembled several hours before the party, then refrigerated until needed. The cake cuts perfectly for individual servings.

YOU WILL NEED:

8 egg whites
2½ cups castor sugar
3 x 300ml cartons thickened cream

To Prepare Trays: Cover two large flat oven trays or scone trays with aluminium foil. On first tray mark two circles, one 15cm (6in), one 10cm (4in) in diameter. On second tray mark three circles, 12cm (5in), 8cm (3in) and 5cm (2in) in diameter. Saucers, cups, jars and lids of the right sizes can be used as guides for circles.

The meringues are made in two batches, each using half of the above ingredients. When ready to make second batch of meringues, cover trays with fresh aluminium foil.

Beat 4 egg whites until soft peaks form. Gradually beat in 1¼ cups of sugar, 1 tablespoon at a time. Make sure each spoonful of sugar is dissolved by beating before adding the next spoonful – this ensures crisp meringues. If you want pink layers in cake, beat in enough food colouring to tint meringue light pink, otherwise leave meringue layers white.

Step 1: Spoon meringue into large piping-bag which has been fitted with a plain tube approximately 2cm (¾in) in diameter. Pipe mixture over circles marked on foil on the two prepared trays; pipe another layer of meringue on top so that each circle is approximately 2cm (¾in) thick.

Step 2: Smooth tops of circles with spatula. Bake both trays in very slow oven 1¼ to 1½ hours. Reverse oven position of slides after 30 minutes cooking time to allow for even cooking. When meringue feels dry to touch, remove from oven and carefully slide foil with meringue circles on top on to cake cooler. Or, if time permits, let meringues cool in oven with door ajar, then slide foil with meringue circles on to cake cooler. Prepare slides as directed above for remaining meringues; mark 18cm (7in) circle on one tray.

Step 3: Prepare second batch of meringue, as above, with remaining 4 egg whites and 1¼ cups of sugar, using no colouring. With piping-bag and same 2cm (¾in) plain tube, pipe a single layer only of meringue over 18cm (7in) circle; mixture should be only about 1cm (½in) thick. Pipe 14 individual meringues approximately 4cm (1½in) in diameter on to foil.

Step 4: Pipe small individual meringues approximately 2.5cm (1in) in diameter on second foil-covered tray. You will need approximately 50 small meringues, which will all fit on to one tray. Put tray with large circle and large meringues on shelf in centre of oven, put tray with small individual meringues on oven shelf beneath. Bake in a very slow oven. After 30 to 45 minutes take lower tray with small meringues from oven and set aside to cool. Move remaining tray one shelf down in the oven (where the small meringues were before). After 45 minutes to 1 hour remove large individual meringues from top tray on to cake cooler. Return large meringue circle to oven for a further 30 minutes cooking time or until it is dry to touch.

Step 5: Whip cream to firm piping consistency, spoon into large piping-bag fitted with star tube. Put 18cm (7in) meringue circle on serving plate, spread top lightly with whipped cream, top with 15cm (6in) circle. Continue with remaining meringue circles in order of size and layers of cream.

Step 6: Pipe circle of cream round bottom layer, gently press 4cm (1½in) diameter individual meringues into circle of cream. Pipe another layer of cream above, press circle of small meringues in place. Continue in this way until all small meringues are used. Pipe small stars of cream in between assembled meringues.

Pavlovas

Pavlova is one of the most popular of all desserts. Here are recipes for the two types of pavlova, the classic and the marshmallow, plus a choice of fillings for the classic pavlova

MARSHMALLOW PAVLOVA SLICE

4 egg whites
1 cup sugar
½ teaspoon vanilla
1 teaspoon white vinegar
1½ cups cream
2 teaspoons sugar, extra
2 punnets strawberries
¼ cup strawberry jam
2 teaspoons brandy

Beat egg whites until soft peaks form, gradually add sugar, beating well after each addition until all sugar is dissolved. Add vanilla and vinegar, beat a further 1 minute. Spread meringue into greased, greased paper lined 28cm by 18cm (11in by 7in) lamington tin which has been lightly dusted with cornflour. Bring paper over sides of tin so it is easy to remove slice when cooked. Bake in slow oven 45 minutes or until meringue is crisp and has a hard shell. Lift out carefully on to wire rack to cool. Trim edges with sharp knife. Beat cream and extra sugar until soft peaks form, spread cream over top and sides of meringue and pipe cream round edges. Wash and hull strawberries, cut each strawberry in half lengthwise, arrange over cream. Put jam and brandy into pan, stir until jam is warm, push through fine sieve, then brush over strawberries. Serves 6.

Note: This is best made and decorated on day of serving but if necessary meringue can be made the day before and topping arranged before serving. This pavlova mixture also can be cooked in a 20cm (8in) springform pan. Line base and sides of pan with lightly greased aluminium foil, dust foil lightly with cornflour. Spread mixture evenly into pan. Bake in slow oven 1½ hours. Turn off heat. Remove pavlova from oven, carefully remove sides of pan. Return pavlova to oven for further 15 minutes. Carefully remove aluminium foil; cool. Decorate as for slice.

CLASSIC PAVLOVA

3 egg whites
pinch salt
¾ cup castor sugar
2 teaspoons cornflour
1 teaspoon lemon juice
extra cornflour

Cut 23cm (9in) circle from piece of greaseproof paper. Place on greased oven tray. Brush lightly with melted butter, dust with extra cornflour. Shake off excess cornflour. Beat egg whites and salt until soft peaks form. Add sugar gradually, beating well after each addition. Beat until sugar is dissolved completely. Lightly fold in sifted cornflour and lemon juice. Spread approximately 5mm (¼in) layer of mixture over prepared circle. Pipe or spoon swirls of remainder of mixture round edge to form shell. Bake in very slow oven 1 hour or until pavlova is dry to touch. Cool in oven.

FILLINGS

FRUIT SALAD and cream is a favourite and colourful filling for a pavlova. But, for a change, try one of these different and delicious fillings.

LEMON FILLING

¾ cup sugar
⅓ cup cornflour
1 cup water
½ cup lemon juice
60g (2oz) butter
3 egg yolks
2 teaspoons gelatine
1 tablespoon water
1 cup cream

Combine sugar and cornflour. Blend in water and lemon juice gradually, stir until smooth. Stir constantly over medium heat until mixture boils and thickens. Remove from heat, quickly stir in butter and egg yolks. Sprinkle gelatine over water, stand over hot water until dissolved. Add to lemon mixture and allow to cool. Lastly fold in lightly whipped cream. Refrigerate 20 minutes, then spoon into pavlova shell; refrigerate until set. Decorate with extra whipped cream.

APRICOT FILLING

30g (1oz) dried apricots
185g (6oz) can apricot nectar
2 tablespoons sugar
2 tablespoons dry white wine
1 teaspoon gelatine
2 teaspoons water
125g (4oz) packaged cream cheese
1 cup cream

Chop apricots. Put in saucepan with nectar, sugar and wine. Stir over heat until sugar dissolves and mixture comes to boil; reduce heat, simmer 10 minutes. Remove from heat, drain, reserve apricots and liquid separately. Sprinkle gelatine over water, stand over hot water until dissolved, add to apricot liquid. Beat cream cheese until smooth, add apricot liquid, fold in reserved apricots. Cool, refrigerate until partly set, then fold in whipped cream. Spoon into pavlova shell, refrigerate until set.

Marshmallow pavlova slice.

Cheesecakes

The popularity of cheesecakes never wanes; there always seems to be a new and even more exciting way of presenting this luscious dessert. Here are some of the most popular, both baked and unbaked

GOURMET CHEESECAKE
BASE
250g (8oz) plain sweet biscuits
125g (4oz) butter
FILLING
375g (12oz) packaged cream cheese
¾ cup castor sugar
1 tablespoon plain flour
pinch salt
2 eggs, separated
1 whole egg, extra
1 cup sour cream
1 tablespoon lemon juice
1 tablespoon castor sugar, extra

Base: Crush biscuits finely, add melted butter, mix well. Press crumb mixture on base and sides of 20cm (8in) springform pan. Refrigerate while preparing filling.
Filling: Beat cream cheese until softened, combine with sugar, flour and salt, beat well. Beat in the whole egg plus the 2 egg yolks, sour cream and lemon juice. Beat egg whites until soft peaks form, beat in extra sugar, fold into cream cheese mixture. Pour into prepared crumb crust. Bake in moderately slow oven 1¼ to 1½ hours. Allow to cool in oven. Refrigerate until firm. If desired, top with 1 cup extra whipped cream, sprinkle with cinnamon or nutmeg.

LEMON MERINGUE CHEESECAKE
BASE
250g (8oz) plain sweet biscuits
125g (4oz) butter
FILLING
250g (8oz) packaged cream cheese
440g (14oz) can sweetened condensed milk
2 eggs, separated
2 teaspoons grated lemon rind
¼ cup lemon juice
½ cup castor sugar

Base: Crush biscuits, mix in melted butter; press into 20cm (8in) springform pan, lining base and bringing crumb mixture three-quarters of way up sides.
Filling: Beat cheese until smooth, beat in condensed milk, lemon rind, lemon juice and egg yolks; pour into prepared crumb crust. Whip egg whites until soft peaks form, gradually beat in half the sugar, beat until stiff, fold in remaining sugar. Spread evenly over filling. Bake in hot oven 10 minutes to brown the meringue. Remove from tin when cold.
Note: Use slightly green lemons for this pie, or mixture will not set firmly.

CHOCOLATE MINT CHEESECAKE
BASE
90g (3oz) plain sweet biscuits
1 tablespoon cocoa
45g (1½oz) butter
FILLING
250g (8oz) packaged cream cheese
⅓ cup sugar
1 teaspoon vanilla
1 teaspoon gelatine
2 teaspoons water
1 cup cream
6 chocolate after-dinner mints
1 tablespoon water, extra

Base: Crush biscuits finely, add cocoa, mix well. Stir in melted butter. Press mixture on to sides and base of greased 18cm (7in) flan tin with removable base. Refrigerate while preparing filling.
Filling: Beat cream cheese, sugar and vanilla until smooth. Sprinkle gelatine over water, dissolve over hot water, cool. Add to cream cheese mixture, beat well, fold in whipped cream. Spoon mixture evenly into crumb crust. Dissolve mints with extra water in top of double saucepan over simmering water; cool a little. Spoon chocolate mint mixture over cream cheese mixture and swirl lightly into mixture with spoon. Refrigerate until set.

BRANDY ALEXANDER CHEESECAKE
BASE
90g (3oz) plain sweet biscuits
60g (2oz) hazelnuts
60g (2oz) butter
60g (2oz) dark chocolate
FILLING
250g (8oz) cottage cheese
250g (8oz) packaged cream cheese
½ cup sugar
1 teaspoon vanilla
2 teaspoons gelatine
2 tablespoons hot water
1 cup cream
2 egg whites
1 tablespoon brandy
1 tablespoon creme de cacao
TOPPING
1 cup cream
1 teaspoon instant coffee powder
1 teaspoon brandy
1 teaspoon creme de cacao
2 teaspoons sugar
nutmeg

Base: Put finely crushed biscuits and finely chopped hazelnuts in basin. Melt butter in pan, add finely chopped chocolate, stir until melted and combined. Add to biscuit mixture; mix well. Press over base of greased 20cm (8in) springform pan. Refrigerate.
Filling: Push cottage cheese through fine sieve. Put cottage cheese and cream cheese into bowl, beat until light and fluffy. Gradually beat in sugar, add vanilla. Dissolve gelatine in hot water, allow to cool. Beat gelatine mixture and unwhipped cream into cream cheese. Beat egg whites until soft peaks form, fold into cream cheese mixture with brandy and creme de cacao. Pour over prepared base. Refrigerate until set. To serve, spoon topping over and pipe it decoratively round edge. Sprinkle with a little grated nutmeg.
Topping: Put all ingredients except nutmeg in bowl, mix lightly, stand 10 minutes. Beat until soft peaks form.

Gourmet cheesecake.

Chocolate mint cheesecake.

Apricot nectar cheesecake.

Cheesecakes

PINEAPPLE-PASSIONFRUIT CHEESECAKE

BASE
125g (4oz) plain sweet biscuits
60g (2oz) butter
1 teaspoon cinnamon
FILLING
250g (8oz) packaged cream cheese
125g (4oz) cottage cheese
½ cup condensed milk
910g (1lb 13oz) can crushed pineapple
4 passionfruit
1 tablespoon gelatine
1½ cups cream
1 passionfruit, extra

Base: Melt butter, crush biscuits finely; combine butter, biscuits and cinnamon, mix well. Lightly grease 20cm (8in) springform pan. Press crumb crust over base only. Refrigerate while preparing filling.

Filling: Drain pineapple, reserve 1 cup of syrup. Put reserved syrup into saucepan, sprinkle gelatine over, stir over low heat until gelatine is dissolved. Refrigerate until almost set. Beat cream cheese, sieved cottage cheese and condensed milk in bowl until very soft and creamy. Gradually add pineapple syrup mixture. Fold in pineapple and passionfruit pulp. Beat half the cream until soft peaks form, fold into cheese mixture. Pour on to prepared base, refrigerate until set. Decorate with remaining whipped cream, swirl extra passionfruit pulp into cream.

Note: This mixture, set in an 18cm by 28cm (7in by 11in) lamington tin, also makes a delightful slice. For this size you will need 185g (6oz) biscuits and 90g (3oz) butter. Line tin with aluminium foil, bringing it over the sides, before pressing crumb crust on the base; this makes it easy to remove

slice when set. Make remainder of recipe as for cheesecake.

APRICOT NECTAR CHEESECAKE

BASE
155g (5oz) plain sweet biscuits
75g (2½oz) butter
FILLING
470g (15oz) can apricot nectar
1 tablespoon gelatine
375g (12oz) packaged cream cheese
½ cup castor sugar
1 tablespoon lemon juice
1 cup cream

Base: Combine finely-crushed biscuit crumbs and melted butter, mix well. Press mixture firmly on to base of 20cm (8in) springform pan, refrigerate while preparing filling.

Filling: Measure 1 cup apricot nectar from can (reserve remainder for topping). Pour nectar into small saucepan, sprinkle gelatine over. Place over low heat and stir until gelatine dissolves; allow to cool and thicken slightly. Beat softened cream cheese and sugar until mixture is smooth and creamy; add lemon juice. Beat in apricot mixture, then fold in whipped cream. Pour mixture into crumb crust, refrigerate 2 hours or until firm.

Topping: Place 1 tablespoon sugar and 3 teaspoons cornflour in saucepan, gradually stir in remaining apricot nectar. Bring mixture to boil, stirring constantly; remove from heat, add 2 teaspoons rum. Continue stirring for a

few minutes to allow mixture to cool slightly. Spread topping over cheesecake, refrigerate until topping sets.

SNOW-WHITE CHEESECAKE

BASE
125g (4oz) plain sweet biscuits
1 teaspoon ground ginger
60g (2oz) butter
TOPPING
250g (8oz) cottage cheese
250g (8oz) packaged cream cheese
½ cup castor sugar
1 teaspoon vanilla
1 tablespoon gelatine
⅓ cup water
1 cup cream
2 egg whites

Base: Crush biscuits finely, add ginger and melted butter. Press evenly over base of greased 20cm (8in) springform pan. Refrigerate while preparing topping.

Topping: Sieve cottage cheese. Beat softened cream cheese until smooth and light; add cottage cheese, sugar and vanilla, beat well. Add gelatine to water, dissolve over hot water; cool. Gradually add unwhipped cream to cheese mixture, beating constantly; add gelatine mixture, beat well. Beat egg whites until soft peaks form, fold into cream cheese mixture. Spread evenly over base, refrigerate until firm. To decorate as shown on back cover, hull and half 1 punnet strawberries, arrange over cheesecake. Heat ¼ cup strawberry jam and 1 tablespoon water until boiling, push through sieve, brush over strawberries to glaze. Pipe around edge with whipped cream. We used tiny loops of choux pastry, dusted with icing sugar, for the decoration.

Pineapple-passionfruit cheesecake.

Pancakes

The family love plain pancakes with sugar and lemon juice. But add a luscious filling and you turn the simple pancake into a superb dessert

PANCAKES
½ cup plain flour
pinch salt
2 eggs
¾ cup milk

Sift dry ingredients into bowl, add eggs, stir until mixture is smooth and free of lumps. Gradually add milk, mixing to a smooth batter. Allow to stand for 30 minutes. Heat pan, grease well. From a small jug pour 2 to 3 tablespoons of pancake mixture into pan, swirling batter evenly around pan. Cook over medium heat until light golden brown. Toss or turn pancake and cook on other side. Repeat with remaining batter. Makes 6 to 8 pancakes.

HAZELNUT PANCAKES
1 quantity pancake batter
185g (6oz) butter
90g (3oz) skinned roasted hazelnuts
1 tablespoon grated orange rind
2 tablespoons orange juice
½ teaspoon cinnamon
1 tablespoon brandy
2 tablespoons sugar
30g (1oz) skinned roasted hazelnuts, extra

Make up pancakes as directed in recipe. Cream butter until light and fluffy, add roughly chopped hazelnuts and remaining ingredients (except extra nuts), mix well. Spread 1 heaped teaspoonful of prepared filling over each pancake, roll up. Put pancakes in small heatproof dish, bake in hot oven 5 to 10 minutes or until pancakes are heated through and butter has begun to melt. If desired, dust with icing sugar;

top with ice-cream, sprinkle with chopped extra nuts. Serves 4.

STRAWBERRY PANCAKES
1 quantity pancake batter
60g (2oz) butter
⅔ cup sugar
1 cup orange juice
¼ cup brandy
2 tablespoons cointreau or grand marnier
2 punnets strawberries
whipped cream

Make up pancakes as directed in recipe. Melt butter in pan, add sugar, stir until combined. Add orange juice, brandy and cointreau, stir over low heat until sugar is dissolved. Bring sauce to boil; boil 5 minutes, remove pan from heat. Hull strawberries, cut in half, reserve 8 strawberry halves for decoration. Add strawberries to pan, stir until coated with liquid. Using slotted spoon, divide strawberries between the pancakes; roll up. Place pancakes on serving plate, spoon over a little of the sauce, top each pancake with whipped cream and decorate with reserved strawberries. Serve with remaining sauce. Serves 4.

PINEAPPLE MERINGUE PANCAKES
1 quantity pancake batter
60g (2oz) butter
1 tablespoon sugar
1 teaspoon grated lemon rind
470g (15oz) can crushed pineapple
1 tablespoon rum
¼ cup water

1 tablespoon cornflour
1 egg white
¼ cup castor sugar

Make up pancakes as directed in recipe. Heat butter in pan, add sugar, stir until sugar is light golden brown. Add lemon rind, undrained pineapple and rum, stir until sugar is dissolved. Combine water and cornflour, gradually add to pineapple, stir until mixture boils and thickens. Simmer uncovered 3 minutes; allow to cool. Spoon approximately 2 tablespoons of pineapple mixture on to one quarter of pancake, fold pancake in half then in half again. Place on heatproof serving plate. Repeat with remaining pancakes. Beat egg white until soft peaks form, gradually add castor sugar, beat until dissolved. Fill meringue into piping bag with star tube attached. Pipe a swirl of meringue on to each pancake. Place in hot oven for 2 minutes or until light golden brown. Serves 6.

ORANGE CREAM PANCAKES
1 quantity pancake batter
250g (8oz) packet cream cheese
½ teaspoon grated orange rind
2 tablespoons sugar
1 egg yolk
60g (2oz) walnuts
⅓ cup sultanas
⅓ cup currants
2 tablespoons mixed peel
⅓ cup sour cream
2 tablespoons grand marnier
apricot jam

Make up pancakes as directed in recipe. Beat cream cheese until soft and creamy, add orange rind, sugar, egg

Hazelnut pancakes.

78

yolk, sour cream and grand marnier; beat well. Fold in chopped walnuts, sultanas, currants and mixed peel. Spread 2 teaspoonfuls of apricot jam down centre of each pancake, divide cream cheese mixture between pancakes; roll up. Put on greased baking tray, bake in moderate oven 10 minutes or until heated through. Serves 4.

PINEAPPLE PASSIONFRUIT PANCAKES
1 quantity pancake batter
2 tablespoons custard powder
¾ cup milk
1 teaspoon vanilla
3 tablespoons sugar
¾ cup cream
2 passionfruit
470g (15oz) can crushed pineapple

Make up pancakes as directed in recipe. Put custard powder and sugar into saucepan, gradually add milk, stir until combined. Add vanilla. Stir over low heat until sauce boils and thickens. Reduce heat, simmer uncovered 2 minutes. Add passionfruit pulp and well-drained pineapple; mix well. Allow custard mixture to cool. Place cream in bowl, beat until soft peaks form, fold into custard mixture, refrigerate until ready to serve. Divide custard mixture evenly between pancakes, roll up. Decorate with whipped cream. Serves 6.

CINNAMON APPLE PANCAKES
1 quantity pancake batter
90g (3oz) butter
⅔ cup brown sugar
2 tablespoons brandy
¾ cup orange juice
1½ teaspoons cinnamon
6 green apples
cream

Make up pancakes as directed in recipe. Melt butter in frying pan, add brown sugar, stir over low heat for 2 minutes. Add brandy and orange juice, stir until sugar is dissolved. Add peeled, cored and sliced apples and cinnamon; simmer gently 3 minutes. Divide apple mixture evenly between pancakes; roll up. Place on serving plates, top with whipped cream. Serves 6.

TIA MARIA BANANAS WITH PANCAKES
1 quantity pancake batter

Pineapple meringue pancakes.

60g (2oz) butter
⅓ cup brown sugar
½ cup orange juice
3 tablespoons tia maria
3 large bananas
cinnamon

Make up pancakes as directed in recipe. Heat butter in large frying pan, add brown sugar, stir until sugar is dissolved and mixture bubbling. Add orange juice, stir until combined. Add tia maria, bring to boil, boil uncovered 3 minutes. Add thickly-sliced bananas, simmer 1 minute. Fold pancakes in half, then in half again. Place on top of bananas, spoon liquid over pancakes until coated. Place 2 pancakes on to each serving plate, spoon over bananas

Strawberry pancakes.

and liquid. Sprinkle lightly with cinnamon. Serve hot with whipped cream. Serves 4.

WALNUT CARAMEL PANCAKES
1 quantity pancake batter
125g (4oz) butter
½ cup brown sugar, lightly packed
1½ tablespoons lemon juice
2 tablespoons water
1 tablespoon brandy
1 teaspoon cinnamon
125g (4oz) walnuts

Make up pancakes as directed in recipe. Melt butter in frying pan, add brown sugar, stir until sugar dissolves and mixture becomes thick. Combine lemon juice, water and brandy, add to sugar-and-butter mixture with cinnamon, mix well. Bring to boil, reduce heat, simmer 2 minutes. Add chopped walnuts. Fold pancakes in half, then in half again. Allow two pancakes for each serving. Put on serving plates, spoon hot sauce over. Top with a scoop of ice-cream. Serves 4.

Biscuits

For afternoon teas, after-dinner coffee, school lunches — there's the perfect biscuit here for each and every occasion

SHORTBREAD BISCUITS
250g (8oz) butter
1 cup icing sugar
1 cup cornflour
1½ cups plain flour
pinch salt

Cream butter and sifted icing sugar until light and fluffy, add sifted flours and salt, mix well. Turn mixture out on to lightly floured board, knead lightly. Divide mixture in half, shape into two rolls approximately 4cm (1½in) wide and 15cm (6in) long. Wrap rolls in plastic food wrap, refrigerate 1 hour or until mixture is firm. Cut into 5mm (¼in) slices, place on oven trays, bake in moderate oven 10 to 15 minutes or until cooked. Makes approximately 40.

ALMOND FRUIT SLICE
3 egg whites
½ cup castor sugar
1 cup plain flour
125g (4oz) unblanched almonds
125g (4oz) glace cherries
60g (2oz) glace pineapple
60g (2oz) glace apricots

Beat egg whites until soft peaks form, gradually beat in castor sugar, beating well after each addition until all sugar is dissolved. Fold in sifted flour, whole unblanched almonds and glace fruits cut into small pieces. Spread into greased 25cm by 8cm (10in by 3in) bar tin. Bake in moderate oven 30 to 35 minutes or until just firm to touch. Turn out of tin to cool. When cold, wrap in aluminium foil, put aside for one or two days. Using very sharp knife, cut bread into wafer-thin slices. Put slices on to oven trays, bake in slow oven 45 minutes or until dry and crisp. Makes approximately 30.

Note: For a simpler, less expensive — but still delicious — biscuit, use only the blanched almonds; omit glace cherries, pineapple and apricots.

DATE AND GINGER SLICE
185g (6oz) dates
125g (4oz) butter
⅓ cup sugar
60g (2oz) preserved ginger
3 cups cornflakes or rice bubbles
125g (4oz) dark chocolate
15g (½oz) solid white vegetable shortening

Put chopped dates, butter, sugar and finely chopped ginger in pan. Stir over low heat until butter has melted and dates are soft. Add cornflakes, mix well. Press mixture into greased and greased paper lined 28cm by 18cm (11in by 7in) lamington tin. Refrigerate until slice is firm. Melt chocolate and vegetable shortening in top of double saucepan over simmering water. Spread chocolate over slice. Return to refrigerator until set. Cut into small squares.

BUTTERSCOTCH MUESLI SQUARES
125g (4oz) butter
1 cup sugar
2 cups packaged unsweetened muesli
1 cup coconut

Melt butter and sugar over low heat; cool. Mix muesli and coconut, add melted butter and sugar, mix well. Press into greased 28cm by 18cm (11in by 7in) lamington tin. Bake in moderate oven 10 to 12 minutes. Cut into squares, allow to cool in tin.

Note: Packaged muesli products vary in their ability to absorb liquid. With most muesli products the 125g (4oz) butter mentioned in ingredients will be sufficient; with others, the completed mixture, ready for baking, may seem dry; in this case, add a further 30g to 60g (1oz to 2oz) melted butter to obtain the correct consistency.

CHOCOLATE PEPPERMINT SLICE
1½ cups self-raising flour
½ cup coconut
½ cup brown sugar
125g (4oz) butter
PEPPERMINT ICING
1¾ cups icing sugar
30g (1oz) solid white vegetable shortening
2 tablespoons milk
½ teaspoon peppermint essence
CHOCOLATE ICING
90g (3oz) solid white vegetable shortening
½ cup drinking chocolate

Sift flour into bowl, add coconut and brown sugar. Add melted butter, mix well. Press into greased 28cm by 18cm (11in by 7in) lamington tin. Bake in moderate oven 20 minutes. While still warm, spread with peppermint icing. When peppermint icing has set, top with chocolate icing.

Peppermint Icing: Melt shortening over gentle heat. Add sifted icing sugar, milk and essence, mix well.

Chocolate Icing: Melt shortening over gentle heat, pour over sifted drinking chocolate, mix well. Cool slightly before spreading on top of peppermint icing. Leave to set, then cut into slices.

Note: It is important when melting solid white vegetable shortening that the mixture is not over-heated. Chop the shortening roughly, then stir over low heat until just melted.

Melting moments.

Biscuits

COCONUT-LEMON MACAROONS

2⅔ cups coconut
1 cup sugar
4 egg whites
1 tablespoon lemon juice
2 teaspoons grated lemon rind
⅓ cup plain flour

In medium pan combine coconut, sugar, 1 egg white, lemon rind and strained lemon juice. Stir over low heat until lukewarm, cool. Beat remaining egg whites until soft peaks form. Gradually fold egg whites into cooled mixture. Add sifted flour, combine gently. Place mixture in heaped teaspoonfuls on to greased oven trays which have been dusted lightly with cornflour. Bake in slow oven 30 minutes. Cool on trays. Makes 15.

GINGERNUTS

125g (4oz) butter
1 cup sugar
2 tablespoons golden syrup

1 egg
2 cups self-raising flour
3 teaspoons ground ginger

Melt butter in pan, remove from heat, add sugar, golden syrup and beaten egg. Mix until well combined. Sift flour and ginger into bowl, pour in butter mixture, mix until combined. Allow to cool a little. Roll teaspoonfuls of mixture into balls. Place well apart on lightly greased oven trays. Bake in moderate oven 12 to 15 minutes. Makes approximately 45.

MELTING MOMENTS

125g (4oz) butter
2 tablespoons icing sugar
½ cup cornflour
½ cup plain flour
125g (4oz) dark chocolate
15g (½oz) solid white vegetable shortening
ORANGE CREAM
30g (1oz) butter
3 tablespoons icing sugar

1 teaspoon grated orange rind
2 teaspoons orange juice

Cream butter and sifted icing sugar together until light and fluffy. Add sifted flours, mix well. Put mixture into piping bag fitted with fluted tube. Pipe small stars on to lightly greased oven trays, bake in moderate oven 10 to 12 minutes until pale golden brown. Cool on trays. Melt chopped chocolate and vegetable shortening over hot water; remove from heat. Dip half of each biscuit into chocolate mixture, place on foil to set. When chocolate has set, join biscuits with orange cream.

Orange Cream: Beat butter until smooth, gradually add sifted icing sugar, beat until mixture is light and creamy. Beat in orange rind and juice. Makes approximately 20 biscuits.

CRISP WHOLEMEAL BISCUITS

1 cup wholemeal plain flour
½ cup soy flour
1 tablespoon sesame seeds
½ teaspoon vegetable salt
2 tablespoons oil
4 tablespoons water, approximately
oil for deep-frying

Put unsifted flours, sesame seeds and salt into bowl, mix lightly. Add oil, mix until oil is distributed evenly through flour. Add water, mix to a soft dough (a little extra water may be needed). Turn on to lightly floured surface, knead 5 minutes. Cover, let stand 15 minutes. Knead again for 5 minutes. Roll dough out on floured surface until paper-thin. Cut into 9cm (3½in) rounds. Put in deep hot oil, fry until golden brown. Serve hot, sprinkled with vegetable salt. Makes approximately 25.

COCONUT OATMEAL COOKIES

1 cup shredded coconut
125g (4oz) butter
1 cup brown sugar, lightly packed
1 egg
1 teaspoon vanilla
1 cup rolled oats
½ cup chopped nuts

Put coconut in shallow pan, stir constantly over heat until coconut is

At left, Almond fruit slice and, at right, Coconut oatmeal cookies.

Biscuits

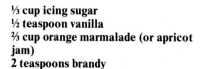

light golden brown. Remove from pan immediately; cool. Cream butter and sugar until light and fluffy, add beaten egg and vanilla, beat well. Stir in oats, nuts and toasted coconut. Drop teaspoonfuls of mixture on to lightly greased and floured oven trays; allow room for spreading. Bake in moderate oven 10 minutes; cool on trays. Makes approximately 30.

DATE AND NUT SLICE
2 eggs
½ cup sugar
15g (½oz) butter
1 tablespoon water
1¼ cups self-raising flour
185g (6oz) dates
¾ cup walnut pieces
LEMON ICING
3 cups icing sugar
15g (½oz) butter
4 tablespoons lemon juice

Beat together eggs and sugar until thick and mousse-like. Combine melted butter and water, add to egg mixture, beat further 1 minute. Stir in sifted flour, roughly chopped dates and walnut pieces. Spoon mixture into greased and greased paper lined 28cm by 18cm (11in by 7in) lamington tin. Bake in moderate oven 25 to 30 minutes or until golden brown on top and cooked through when tested with a skewer. When cool, top with Lemon Icing. Allow icing to set before cutting into fingers.

Lemon Icing: Sift icing sugar into bowl, add softened butter and lemon juice, beat until mixture is smooth.

ORANGE BRANDY CREAM BISCUITS
125g (4oz) butter
3 tablespoons castor sugar
1 teaspoon grated orange rind
1 egg yolk
1⅓ cups plain flour
FILLING
125g (4oz) butter
⅓ cup icing sugar
½ teaspoon vanilla
⅔ cup orange marmalade (or apricot jam)
2 teaspoons brandy

Cream butter, sugar and orange rind until very light and creamy, add egg yolk, beat well. Lightly fold in sifted flour until just combined. Form pastry into ball, wrap in plastic food wrap and refrigerate 1 hour. Turn on to well-floured surface, knead lightly. Roll out pastry to 3mm (⅛in) thickness. Cut into 5cm (2in) rounds with fluted pastry cutter. Cut out a small fluted circle from centre of half these rounds. Place on greased oven trays. Bake in moderately slow oven 12 to 15 minutes or until light golden brown; cool. Put filling into piping bag fitted with a small fluted tube. Pipe a band of cream round edges of biscuits that do not have a hole. Spoon a little jam in the centre of the cream, top with holed biscuit. Dust with extra icing sugar.

Filling: Beat butter until soft and creamy, add sifted icing sugar, beat until smooth. Add vanilla. Push marmalade through fine sieve, add brandy, mix well.

ALMOND FINGERS
1½ cups plain flour
½ cup self-raising flour
3 tablespoons sugar
125g (4oz) butter
1 egg, separated
2 tablespoons milk, approximately
1 cup icing sugar
90g (3oz) slivered almonds

Sift flours into bowl, add sugar, mix well. Rub in butter until mixture comes together. Add egg yolk and enough of the milk to mix to a firm dough. Roll out to a square 30cm by 30cm (12in by 12in), trim edges. Beat egg white lightly, stir in sifted icing sugar. Spread over the dough and sprinkle with roughly chopped almonds. Cut into fingers 2.5cm by 5cm (1in by 2in), place on greased oven trays, bake in moderately slow oven 20 to 25 minutes or until lightly browned. Remove from trays while warm. Makes approximately 40.

At left, Date and nut slice and, right, Almond fingers and Gingernuts.

Breads & Scones

Nothing tastes quite as good as home-made bread, fresh from the oven — unless it is hot scones, spread with butter

MILK LOAF

1kg (2lb) plain flour
1 tablespoon salt
60g (2oz) compressed yeast
3 tablespoons sugar
470g (15oz) can evaporated milk
2 cups water
60g (2oz) butter
2 eggs

Sift flour and salt into bowl. Put yeast into second bowl, add sugar, stir until mixture is combined. Put evaporated milk and water into pan, stand over heat until lukewarm; remove from heat, gradually add to yeast mixture. Sprinkle 1 tablespoon of the sifted flour over the yeast mixture, cover bowl, stand in warm place until frothy, approximately 10 minutes. Make a large well in centre of dry ingredients, add yeast mixture, melted butter and well-beaten eggs, mix to a soft dough. Turn out on to well floured surface; knead for 2 minutes. Place dough in large oiled bowl, cover and stand in warm place for 45 minutes or until doubled in bulk. Turn out on to floured surface, knead for 5 minutes or until dough is smooth. Divide dough into 4 equal portions. Knead each portion well and form into loaf shape. Put into 4 well-greased 20cm by 10cm (8in by 4in) loaf tins. Cover and let rise until dough reaches tops of tins. Brush tops of dough with water. Bake in hot oven 30 to 35 minutes. Turn out and cool on wire racks. Makes 4 loaves.

FRENCH BREAD

½ cup milk
1 cup water
2 teaspoons sugar
30g (1oz) butter
30g (1oz) compressed yeast
4 cups plain flour
2 teaspoons salt
1 egg yolk
1 teaspoon water, extra
sesame seeds

Place milk, water, sugar and butter in pan, stand over low heat until butter is melted, allow to become lukewarm. Add yeast, stir until yeast is dissolved. Sift flour and salt into large bowl, make a well in centre of dry ingredients, add milk mixture, sprinkle over a little flour from sides of bowl. Stand bowl in warm place until milk mixture is frothy. Mix in flour, turn out on to floured surface; knead well. Place dough in lightly oiled bowl, cover, stand in warm place until doubled in bulk, approximately 20 minutes. Punch down, knead on floured surface for 3 minutes. Return to bowl, place in warm place until doubled in bulk; approximately 20 minutes. Turn out on to floured surface, knead well. Divide mixture into 6 equal portions. Roll each portion into roll 40cm (16in) long. Take three rolls and form into plait, securing at each end. Repeat with remaining rolls. Place on large greased oven tray. Place in warm place until doubled in bulk. Brush plaits with combined egg yolk and extra water,

sprinkle over sesame seeds. Bake in hot oven 20 to 25 minutes or until bread sounds hollow when tapped on base. Makes 2 loaves.

CONTINENTAL RYE BREAD

4 cups rye plain flour
4 cups plain flour
1 tablespoon salt
30g (1oz) compressed yeast
½ cup lukewarm milk
1 tablespoon sugar
1 tablespoon coriander seeds
1 tablespoon caraway seeds
1 tablespoon aniseed seeds
1 tablespoon lemon juice
2¼ cups lukewarm water

Sift flours and salt into basin; mix well. Put yeast into small bowl, add lukewarm milk and sugar, stir until yeast is dissolved. Cover bowl, stand in warm place until mixture appears frothy on surface. Crush coriander seeds, add to flour mixture with remaining seeds; mix well. Make well in centre of flour mixture, add yeast mixture, water and lemon juice, mix with hands until mixture is well combined. (A little extra warm water may be needed). Put dough into large bowl that has been lightly greased with oil. Cover, stand in warm place until doubled in bulk; approximately 20 minutes. Punch down, knead on lightly floured surface for 5 minutes. Divide dough into 4 equal portions. Knead

Continental rye bread and, right, French bread.

88

each portion into a round. Place two rounds side by side in greased 23cm by 12cm (9in by 5in) loaf tin. Do the same with remaining rounds. Place both tins in warm place until dough has risen to tops of tins. Brush with water. Cook in hot oven 30 to 35 minutes. Makes 2.

FRUIT LOAF
4 cups plain flour
2 teaspoons salt
1 teaspoon cinnamon
1 teaspoon mixed spice
2 tablespoons sugar
30g (1oz) compressed yeast
½ cup milk
¾ cup water
1 egg
30g (1oz) butter
250g (8oz) mixed fruit
1 egg yolk
2 tablespoons water, extra

Sift flour, salt, cinnamon and mixed spice into large bowl; mix in fruit. Place yeast in small bowl, add sugar, stir until combined. Add lukewarm water and milk to yeast mixture, stir until combined. Sprinkle 1 tablespoon of the sifted flour over yeast mixture. Cover bowl, stand in warm place until frothy. Make a well in centre of dry ingredients, add beaten egg, yeast mixture and melted butter; mix well. Place dough in clean bowl, which has been greased lightly with oil. Cover bowl, stand in warm place until mixture has· doubled in bulk. Turn out on to floured surface, knead well. Divide mixture in half. Knead each half into smooth oblong shape. Place in two greased 20cm by 10cm (8in by 4in) loaf tins. Cover tins, stand in warm place until dough reaches tops of tins. Brush tops of dough with combined beaten egg yolk and extra water. Bake in

moderately hot oven 30 to 35 minutes. Remove from tins, cool on wire rack. Makes 2.

WHOLEMEAL DATE SCONES
1½ cups wholemeal self-raising flour
1 cup white self-raising flour
pinch salt
¼ teaspoon nutmeg
1 teaspoon cinnamon
½ teaspoon grated lemon rind
60g (2oz) butter
125g (4oz) dates
2 tablespoons honey
½ cup milk
1 egg

Sift dry ingredients into bowl; add lemon rind. Rub in butter until mixture resembles fine breadcrumbs. Add chopped dates, mix lightly. Make a well in centre, add combined honey, egg and milk, mix to a soft dough. Turn out on to lightly floured surface, knead lightly. Pat out dough to 2cm (¾in) thickness, cut into rounds with 5cm (2in) cutter. Place on greased oven tray. Glaze tops with extra milk. Bake in hot oven 12 to 15 minutes. Makes approximately 15.

CINNAMON SUGAR SCONES
2 cups self-raising flour
pinch salt
90g (3oz) butter
⅔ cup milk
2 tablespoons sugar
1 teaspoon cinnamon
30g (1oz) butter, extra

Sift flour and salt into bowl, rub in butter until mixture resembles fine breadcrumbs. Add milk, mix to a soft dough. Turn on to floured surface, knead lightly. Roll out to 5mm (¼in) thickness; cut into rounds using 9cm (3½in) cutter. Brush with melted extra butter. Fold in half. Brush top and sides with melted butter. Sprinkle tops thickly with combined sugar and cinnamon. Place on lightly greased oven tray, sugar side uppermost. Bake in hot oven 10 to 15 minutes. Makes approximately 12.

Left: Cinnamon sugar scones and, at back, Wholemeal date scones. Right: Fruit loaf.

Sweet Pies

These pies will be great favourites with all ages

PINEAPPLE-PASSIONFRUIT PIE
PASTRY
1 cup plain flour
1 tablespoon sugar
90g (3oz) butter
1 egg yolk
2 teaspoons water
FILLING
470g (15oz) can crushed pineapple
2 strips lemon rind
¼ cup lemon juice
3 tablespoons custard powder
1 egg yolk
2 passionfruit

Pastry: Sift flour and sugar into bowl, rub in butter until mixture resembles fine breadcrumbs. Add combined beaten egg yolk and water, mix to firm dough. Turn pastry on to lightly floured surface, roll out to fit base and sides of 23cm (9in) flan tin. Trim edges of pastry, prick base and sides with fork. Bake in moderately hot oven 12 to 15 minutes or until pastry is cooked and golden brown; cool.

Filling: Drain crushed pineapple, reserve syrup; add enough water to syrup to measure 1 cup. Put liquid into pan, add lemon rind, lemon juice and custard powder, blend until smooth. Stir until sauce boils and thickens. Remove from heat, discard lemon rind; stir in lightly beaten egg yolk, passionfruit pulp and drained pineapple; cool. Spread cooled filling over base of pastry case, top with meringue, bake in moderate oven 3 to 5 minutes or until meringue is set and golden brown.

Meringue: Beat two egg whites in bowl until firm peaks form, gradually add ⅓ cup castor sugar, beating well after each addition; beat until sugar has dissolved.

APPLE PIE
PASTRY
1½ cups plain flour
¾ cup self-raising flour
⅓ cup custard powder
⅓ cup cornflour
pinch salt
185g (6oz) butter
1 tablespoon sugar
1 egg yolk
3 tablespoons water (approximately)
1 egg white for glazing
extra sugar
FILLING
7 large cooking apples
½ teaspoon grated lemon rind
3 tablespoons sugar
½ cup water
2 tablespoons apricot jam

Pastry: Sift flours, custard powder and salt into basin. Rub in butter until mixture resembles fine breadcrumbs, add sugar; mix well. Make well in centre of dry ingredients, add egg yolk and water, mix to a firm dough, knead lightly. Refrigerate pastry 1 hour. Roll out just over half the pastry, line a 23cm (9in) pie plate. Spread base of pie with apricot jam. Put cooled and drained apple over apricot jam. Roll out remaining pastry, brush edges of pie with milk and cover with pastry. Press edges together firmly, trim and decorate. Brush top with lightly-beaten egg white, sprinkle with extra sugar. Cut a few slits in top. Bake in moderately hot oven 20 minutes, reduce heat to moderate, cook further 20 to 25 minutes or until pie is golden brown.

Filling: Peel, quarter and core apples; cut each quarter in half lengthways. Put in saucepan with water, sugar and lemon rind. Cook, covered, until apples are almost tender and still holding shape. Remove from heat, drain off syrup; allow apples to cool.

FRUIT PIE
PASTRY
185g (6oz) butter
½ cup sugar
2 eggs
2 cups plain flour
½ cup self-raising flour
pinch salt
1 egg yolk for glazing
extra sugar
FILLING
250g (8oz) dates
2 teaspoons grated lemon rind
¼ cup lemon juice
125g (4oz) sultanas
125g (4oz) raisins
30g (1oz) mixed peel
60g (2oz) glace cherries
60g (2oz) butter
1 teaspoon mixed spice
1 cup water
1 tablespoon arrowroot
1 tablespoon rum or orange juice

Pastry: Beat butter until soft, add sugar, beat only until combined. Add beaten eggs gradually, beat until combined. Overcreaming at this stage will result in a pastry which will be soft and difficult to handle. Add half of sifted dry ingredients to creamed mixture, stir in until combined, add remaining dry ingredients, mix with wooden spoon until too stiff to stir, then use hands to combine. Refrigerate 30 minutes. Roll out two-thirds pastry on lightly floured board to fit greased 20cm (8in) pie plate, spread filling in evenly. Roll out remaining pastry, fit on top of pie, trim and decorate edges. Brush top of pie with beaten egg yolk and sprinkle with a little sugar. Bake in moderately hot oven 30 to 35 minutes or until golden brown. This is nice served warm with cream or ice-cream or with Brandy Custard (see Index for recipe). It would make an ideal fruit mince pie for Christmas.

Filling: Put into saucepan chopped fruit and all ingredients except arrowroot and rum or orange juice. Stir constantly over heat until butter melts and mixture becomes thick, remove from heat. Blend arrowroot with rum or orange juice, stir into fruit mixture. Return to heat, stir until mixture boils, reduce heat, simmer 1 minute. Cool.

Fruit pie.

Sweet Pies

STRAWBERRY CREAM PIE

125g (4oz) plain sweet biscuits
60g (2oz) butter
125g (4oz) packet cream cheese
½ cup sugar
1 teaspoon vanilla
3 eggs
½ cup cream
½ cup milk
1 punnet strawberries
¼ cup strawberry jam
1 tablespoon water

Put finely crushed biscuits into bowl, add melted butter; mix well. Put two wide strips of greased greaseproof paper over base and sides of deep 20cm (8in) round cake tin. Cover the base of the tin with a circle of aluminium foil. Press prepared biscuit crumb over base. Refrigerate while preparing filling. Beat cream cheese until soft and creamy, add sugar, beat well. Add eggs one at a time, beating well after each addition. Add milk, cream and vanilla, beat until combined. Pour mixture over biscuit base. Cook in moderately slow oven for 45 minutes or until custard is set. Allow to cool then refrigerate until well chilled. To turn out, place base of cake tin in hot water for a few seconds, lift pie on to serving plate. Arrange hulled, halved strawberries over top. Stir strawberry jam and water over low heat until smooth. Push through sieve. Brush glaze over strawberries. Decorate with whipped cream.

RHUBARB PIE

PASTRY
1½ cups plain flour
¾ cup self-raising flour
⅓ cup cornflour
⅓ cup custard powder
pinch salt
185g (6oz) butter
1 tablespoon sugar
1 egg yolk
3 tablespoons water
1 egg white for glazing
extra sugar
FILLING
1kg (2lb) rhubarb, approx. 10 sticks
3 cooking apples
½ cup water
¾ cup sugar
½ teaspoon ground ginger
3 tablespoons arrowroot
3 tablespoons water, extra
3 passionfruit

Pastry: Sift flours, custard powder and salt into basin. Rub in butter until mixture resembles fine breadcrumbs, add sugar, mix well. Make hollow in centre of dry ingredients, add egg yolk and water (a little more water may be necessary), mix to a firm dough. Turn on to lightly floured surface, knead lightly, roll in greaseproof paper, refrigerate 1 hour. Roll out just over half the pastry, line 23cm (9in) pie plate. Fill with cooled filling. Roll out remaining pastry, brush edges of pie with milk, cover with pastry. Press edges

together firmly, trim and decorate. Brush top with lightly beaten egg white, sprinkle with extra sugar. Bake in moderately hot oven 15 minutes, reduce heat to moderate for 20 to 25 minutes.

Filling: Wash and trim rhubarb, cut into 2.5cm (1in) pieces. Put into saucepan with peeled, cored and finely sliced apples, water, sugar and ginger. Bring slowly to boil, reduce heat, simmer 5 minutes or until rhubarb is cooked. Blend arrowroot with extra water, add to saucepan, stir until mixture boils. Remove from heat, add passionfruit pulp. Allow to cool.

TOFFEE-CREAM PIE

CRUMB CRUST
125g (4oz) plain sweet biscuit crumbs
60g (2oz) butter
FILLING
3 eggs, separated
½ cup sugar
½ cup sugar, extra
¼ cup water
3 teaspoons gelatine
1 tablespoon water, extra
1 tablespoon brandy
1 teaspoon vanilla
1 cup cream
1 cup cream, extra

Crumb crust: Combine finely crushed biscuits and melted butter, mix well. Press into base and sides of 20cm (8in) greased pie plate, refrigerate while preparing filling.

Filling: Beat egg yolks and sugar until light and creamy. Cook in top of double saucepan over simmering water until sugar has dissolved and mixture is thick and creamy. Put extra sugar and water in saucepan, stir over low heat until sugar has dissolved, increase heat, boil without stirring until toffee turns light golden brown. Pour toffee mixture into hot egg yolk mixture, stirring constantly; continue stirring over hot water until mixture is smooth and toffee has combined evenly, remove from heat. Sprinkle gelatine over extra water, dissolve over hot water, add to hot toffee mixture with brandy and vanilla, cool. Fold in whipped cream and softly beaten egg whites, spoon evenly into crumb crust, refrigerate until set. Decorate with extra whipped cream.

**Left: Strawberry cream pie.
Right: Toffee-cream pie.**

Savoury Pies

Here's a selection of hearty pies for the daily menu and special occasions

CURRY PUFFS
250g (8oz) minced steak
salt, pepper
1 tablespoon soy sauce
1 tablespoon oil
1 onion
1 tablespoon grated green ginger
1 tablespoon curry powder
1 teaspoon cornflour
2 tablespoons water
1 beef stock cube
375g (12oz) pkt puff pastry
oil for deep-frying

Combine minced steak, salt, pepper and soy sauce, mix well. Heat oil in pan, saute peeled and finely chopped onion and green ginger until onion is transparent. Stir in curry powder, cook 1 minute. Add meat mixture to pan, stir until meat is well browned; drain off excess fat. Blend cornflour with water, add to meat mixture with crumbled stock cube, cook further 1 minute; allow to cool. Roll out pastry very thinly on lightly floured surface, cut into rounds with 8cm (3in) cutter. Put a teaspoonful of mixture on to each round, glaze edges of pastry with water, fold in half, press edges together. Deep-fry in hot oil until golden. Drain on absorbent paper. Makes 24. These can be served with drinks, with Ginger Chutney for dipping. Heat 1 cup fruit chutney, 1 teaspoon grated green ginger and 1 teaspoon soy sauce.

PIZZA
YEAST DOUGH
30g (1oz) compressed yeast
1 teaspoon sugar
1 cup lukewarm water
3 cups plain flour
½ teaspoon salt
4 tablespoons oil
FILLING
1 tablespoon oil
1 onion
2 cloves garlic
2 x 470g (15oz) cans whole tomatoes
3 tablespoons tomato paste
1 teaspoon oregano
1 teaspoon basil
2 teaspoons sugar
salt, pepper
TOPPING
250g (8oz) mozzarella cheese
4 tablespoons grated parmesan cheese
2 x 60g (2oz) cans anchovy fillets
125g (4oz) black olives
60g (2oz) mushrooms
1 small green pepper
4 tablespoons oil

Filling: Make filling first. Heat oil in pan, add peeled and finely chopped onion. Saute until onion is transparent. Add crushed garlic, cook for 1 minute, stirring constantly. Stir in undrained tomatoes and remaining ingredients. Season with salt and pepper. Bring sauce to boil, reduce heat and simmer uncovered, stirring occasionally, app-roximately 30 to 40 minutes or until sauce is thick and smooth. Cool.

Yeast Dough: Cream yeast with sugar, add lukewarm water, let stand 10 minutes or until bubbles appear on surface. Sift flour and salt into bowl, make a well in centre, add oil and yeast mixture. Mix to a firm dough with hands. Turn dough out on to floured surface, knead for 15 minutes or until dough is smooth and elastic. Place dough in lightly oiled bowl, cover; place in warm place 30 minutes or until dough has doubled in bulk. Knock dough down, divide into half, knead each half into a ball. Flatten dough into a circle about 2.5cm (1in) thick. Roll out from centre to edge to fit 25cm (10in) pizza pan or 30cm by 25cm (12in by 10in) swiss roll tin. Repeat with remaining dough. Divide filling in half, spread evenly over each pizza with back of spoon. (The pizza in swiss roll tin can be cut into small squares when cooked and served with drinks).

Topping: Combine grated mozzarella cheese and grated parmesan cheese, sprinkle over pizzas. Top with well-drained anchovy fillets, finely chopped pepper and finely sliced mushrooms. Sprinkle with halved olives. Spoon 2 tablespoons oil over each pizza to prevent drying out in cooking. Bake in hot oven 10 to 15 minutes until crust is golden brown.

Curry puffs.

Savoury Pies

Tomato-anchovy quiche.

TOMATO-ANCHOVY QUICHE
PASTRY
1 cup plain flour
salt
90g (3oz) butter
1 egg yolk
2 teaspoons water
FILLING
60g (2oz) butter
1 onion
1 clove garlic
2 x 470g (15oz) cans whole peeled tomatoes
salt, pepper
1 teaspoon sugar
1 teaspoon basil
2 tablespoons finely chopped parsley
60g (2oz) can anchovies
3 eggs
1 tablespoon grated parmesan cheese
60g (2oz) cheese

Pastry: Sift flour and salt into bowl, rub in butter until mixture resembles fine breadcrumbs. Add combined beaten egg yolk and water, mix to a firm dough. Roll pastry on lightly floured surface to fit 23cm (9in) flan tin, trim edges, prick base and sides with fork. Bake in moderately hot oven 12 to 15 minutes or until cooked; cool.

Filling: Heat butter in pan, saute peeled and finely chopped onion and crushed garlic until onion is transparent. Add undrained, mashed tomatoes. Add salt, pepper, sugar, basil and parsley, bring to boil, reduce heat, simmer uncovered 45 minutes, stirring occasionally; the mixture at this stage should be quite thick. Drain anchovies, add anchovy oil to tomato sauce; chop anchovies finely, add to sauce, mix well; cool. Beat eggs and parmesan cheese, mix into tomato sauce. Spoon filling evenly into pastry case, sprinkle with grated cheese. Bake in moderately slow oven 35 to 40 minutes or until cooked. Serves 4 to 6.

BEEF AND BURGUNDY PIE
1.25kg (2½lb) round steak
1 tablespoon oil
60g (2oz) butter
2 onions
1 clove garlic
2 carrots
125g (4oz) mushrooms
3 rashers bacon
30g (1oz) butter, extra
2 tablespoons flour
1½ cups water
½ cup burgundy or claret
2 beef stock cubes
1 teaspoon sugar
salt, pepper
375g (12oz) packaged puff pastry
1 egg yolk
1 tablespoon milk

Remove fat from meat, cut meat into 2.5cm (1in) cubes. Heat oil and butter in large pan, saute meat until well browned; do this in two batches so meat browns well; remove from pan. Peel and dice onions; crush garlic; peel and dice carrots; slice mushrooms; dice bacon. Add all vegetables and bacon to pan, saute until golden brown, remove from pan. Melt extra butter in pan, stir in flour, stir until golden brown, remove from heat, add water, wine, crumbled stock cubes, sugar, salt and pepper. Return to heat, stir until sauce boils and thickens. Reduce heat, simmer 2 minutes. Return meat and vegetables to pan, cover, simmer until meat is tender,

Beef and burgundy pie.

approximately 1¼ hours; cool. When cold, divide filling between four individual ovenproof dishes. Divide pastry into 4 equal portions. Roll out each portion slightly larger than the ovenproof dishes. Glaze edges of dishes with combined beaten egg yolk and milk. Cut thin strips from pastry and fit round moistened edges. Brush pastry rim with egg glaze, put remaining pastry on top. Press edges together, trim off excess pastry; make 2 slits in top of pastry to allow steam to escape. Glaze tops with egg yolk glaze. Put dishes on oven tray, bake in hot oven 10 minutes, reduce heat to moderately hot, bake further 20 to 25 minutes or until pastry is golden brown. Serves 4.

Note: Of course, if preferred, the same mixture can be used to make one family-size pie instead of four individual pies.

CURRIED CHICKEN PIE
1.5kg (3lb) chicken
2 large carrots
1 large parsnip
3 medium potatoes
1 cup frozen peas
60g (2oz) butter
2 teaspoons curry powder
3 tablespoons plain flour
½ cup cream
salt, pepper
250g (8oz) pkt puff pastry
1 egg yolk
1 tablespoon water

Steam or boil chicken in usual way until tender; reserve 3 cups of the chicken stock. Put chopped carrots, peeled and sliced parsnip, peeled and quartered potatoes into saucepan, add reserved stock. Bring to boil, reduce heat. Simmer, covered, 15 minutes or until vegetables are just tender, add peas. Drain vegetables, reserve stock. Heat butter in separate saucepan, add curry powder and flour, stir until combined, remove from heat. Add 2 cups of reserved stock and cream, stir until combined. Return pan to heat, stir until sauce boils and thickens, reduce heat, simmer uncovered 2 minutes. Season with salt and pepper. Remove skin and bones from chicken, cut chicken into large pieces. Put chicken, sauce and vegetables into bowl; mix well, allow to cool. Spoon chicken into deep pie dish. Brush edges of dish with a little milk. Roll out pastry to cover dish, pressing edges firmly on to dish. Trim edges. Combine egg yolk and water, brush over pastry. Make a slit in top of pastry. Bake in very hot oven 10 minutes or until golden, reduce heat to moderate, cook further 25 minutes. Serves 4 to 6.

Cold Desserts

Light, luscious desserts provide a happy ending to a substantial meal. They're perfect for dinner parties or for when you want something deliciously different

CHOCOLATE PEARS WITH LIQUEUR

6 pears
1½ cups dry white wine
1½ cups water
¾ cup sugar
4 strips orange rind
8cm (3in) cinnamon stick
2 tablespoons grand marnier
125g (4oz) milk chocolate
125g (4oz) dark chocolate

Peel pears, leaving stems on. Trim bases of pears so that pears stand upright. Place wine, water, orange rind, sugar and cinnamon stick in pan, stir over low heat until sugar has dissolved. Add pears, cover, simmer gently 20 minutes or until pears are just tender. Allow pears to cool in liquid. Remove pears from liquid; reserve liquid. Add grand marnier to liquid, cover, refrigerate. Put pears in refrigerator until cold. Put milk chocolate and dark chocolate in top of double saucepan, stand over simmering water until chocolate has melted. Allow chocolate to cool, until it is just warm. Gently pat pears with absorbent paper to remove excess moisture. Dip pears into chocolate to coat pears completely. Remove pears from chocolate and, holding on to stems gently so that stems do not break, drain off excess chocolate. Place on aluminium foil. Refrigerate until ready to serve. Pour the chilled liquid into individual dishes, put a pear in each dish. Serves 6.

MANGOES WITH COINTREAU ICE

850g can mango slices
⅓ cup sugar
2 cups water
½ cup orange juice
¼ cup cointreau

Combine sugar, water and orange juice. Stir over medium heat until sugar has dissolved. Cool. Strain, add cointreau, pour into freezer tray, freeze. Drain mangoes, put mango slices into serving glasses or dishes: flake ice with fork, spoon on top of mango slices.

Note: Fresh ripe mangoes can be substituted for the canned fruit. Allow one medium mango, cut into slices, for each person. Serves 4.

CREME BRULEE

6 egg yolks
4 tablespoons castor sugar
½ teaspoon vanilla
2½ cups cream
2 tablespoons castor sugar, extra
2 tablespoons brown sugar

Place egg yolks, sugar and vanilla in bowl, beat until thick and creamy. Place cream in pan, stir over heat until almost to the boil. Remove from heat immediately. Add cream to egg yolk mixture, beat until combined. Pour cream mixture into top of double saucepan. Stir over simmering water until mixture lightly coats back of wooden spoon, approximately 3 minutes. Remove from heat immediately. Pour into shallow heatproof dish. Bake in slow oven 30 minutes. Remove from oven, cool. Refrigerate several hours or overnight. Combine extra sugar and brown sugar. Sift this mixture evenly over custard. Preheat griller until very hot, place dish under, cook until sugar melts, approximately 1 to 2 minutes. Watch carefully: the sugar will burn easily. Remove from heat, allow to cool, then refrigerate until custard is set again and topping is firm. Serve with fresh fruit. Delicious spooned over mangoes sprinkled with rum or strawberries with grand marnier or cointreau. Serves 4 to 6.

RUM BAVARIAN SLICE

BASE
90g (3oz) dark chocolate
30g (1oz) butter
1 tablespoon sugar
1 egg
1 tablespoon milk
1½ cups crushed cornflakes
½ cup coconut
TOPPING
4 eggs, separated
½ cup sugar
2 teaspoons gelatine
1 tablespoon water
1½ tablespoons rum
1½ cups cream
60g (2oz) dark chocolate, extra

Base: Put chopped chocolate, butter and sugar in top of double saucepan. Stir over simmering water until chocolate and butter have melted. Add combined beaten egg and milk, stir until well combined. Remove from heat. When cold, fold in cornflakes and coconut. Press mixture evenly into 28cm by 18cm (11in by 7in) lamington tin lined with aluminium foil. Refrigerate while preparing topping.

Topping: Sprinkle gelatine over water, stand over hot water until dissolved. Beat egg yolks and sugar until pale and fluffy. Put in top of double saucepan over simmering water, stir until sugar dissolves and mixture

Cherries with rose wine.

becomes thick. Remove from heat, add dissolved gelatine and rum, mix well, let cool slightly. Fold in whipped cream, then softly beaten egg whites. Spoon mixture evenly over base, refrigerate until set. Before serving, drizzle top of slice with extra melted chocolate. Decorate each serving, if desired, with whipped cream and a strawberry.

STRAWBERRY WATER ICE

1 punnet strawberries
1 cup water
½ cup castor sugar
2 tablespoons lemon juice
2 tablespoons grand marnier or cointreau

Put water, sugar, lemon juice and grand marnier or cointreau into electric blender. Add washed and hulled strawberries. Blend on medium speed 2 minutes. Push strawberry mixture through fine sieve into 28cm by 18cm (11in by 7in) lamington tin. Freeze. When ready to serve, remove from freezer. Run fork across ice so that it flakes and separates. Fork into individual serving glasses. It's a good idea to refrigerate glasses for an hour or so beforehand. The ice will not melt as quickly in cold glasses. Serves 6.

MANGO AND LIME MOUSSE

3 eggs, separated
½ cup sugar
2 teaspoons gelatine
1 tablespoon water
⅓ cup fresh lime or lemon juice
¼ cup dry white wine
2 teaspoons creme de menthe
850g can mango slices
1 cup cream

Beat egg yolks and sugar until light and creamy. Stir in top of double saucepan over simmering water until sugar dissolves and mixture is thick. Sprinkle gelatine over water, dissolve over hot water, add to egg yolk mixture, remove from heat. Add lime or lemon juice, white wine, creme de menthe; cool. Add drained and mashed mangoes. Then fold in whipped cream and softly beaten egg whites. Spoon mixture into large serving dish or six individual dishes, refrigerate until set. Decorate with extra whipped cream and slices of lime or lemon. Serves 6.

CHERRIES WITH ROSE WINE

2 x 470g (15oz) cans cherries
¼ cup sugar
1 cup water
2 cups rose wine

Drain cherries, reserve syrup. Put sugar and water into saucepan, stir over low heat until sugar dissolves. Bring to boil; reduce heat, simmer 5 minutes. Remove from heat, cool. Add wine and ¾ cup of reserved cherry syrup. Pour into two freezer trays, freeze overnight. Combine cherries and remaining syrup in bowl; cover, refrigerate until serving time. To serve, put cherries in individual glasses, pour over some of the syrup. Flake ice with fork, spoon over cherries. Serves 4.

MARSALA ICE-CREAM

3 eggs, separated
½ cup sugar
1 cup cream
2 tablespoons marsala (or cointreau or grand marnier)
2 tablespoons water

Put egg yolks, sugar, marsala and water in heatproof bowl. Beat over hot water until mixture is lukewarm. Remove from heat, beat until fluffy and cool, approximately 10 minutes. Whip cream until firm, fold into marsala mixture. Whip egg whites until soft peaks form, fold into marsala mixture. Spoon mixture into deep 20cm (8in) tin. Cover with aluminium foil, freeze until firm, stirring occasionally to combine marsala and cream mixture. Delicious served as an accompaniment to Chocolate Souffle (see Index). Serves 4.

RUM FRUITS

4 kiwi fruit (chinese gooseberries)
1 pineapple
1 punnet strawberries
60g (2oz) preserved ginger
1½ tablespoons rum
2 tablespoons sugar
3 tablespoons water
5cm (2in) cinnamon stick

Peel kiwi fruit, cut into slices. Peel the pineapple, cut into chunks. Remove stems from strawberries, leave whole. Slice ginger. Arrange fruit in four individual serving dishes. Put rum, sugar, water and cinnamon stick in small saucepan, stir over low heat until

Chocolate pears with liqueur.

Rum Bavarian slice.

Creme brulee.

Cold Desserts

sugar dissolves. Remove cinnamon stick, pour syrup over the fruit. Serve with a bowl of whipped cream. Serves 4.

STRAWBERRY MOUSSE

1 punnet strawberries
½ cup castor sugar
1¼ cups cream
1 tablespoon lemon juice
⅓ cup boiling water
2 teaspoons gelatine
2 egg whites

Place washed and hulled strawberries, sugar, lemon juice and cream into electric blender. Place boiling water into small bowl, add gelatine, stir until dissolved. Add to strawberries in blender. Blend on medium speed for 30 seconds or until mixture is just combined. Beat egg whites in bowl until soft peaks form, add strawberry mixture, stir until combined. Pour mixture into four individual serving dishes. Refrigerate until firm. Serves 4.

CHOCOLATE CHESTNUT CREAM

280g (9oz) can chestnut puree
2 tablespoons brandy
1 cup cream
2 tablespoons sugar
60g (2oz) dark chocolate
¼ cup flaked almonds

Beat chestnut puree and brandy until smooth. Beat cream and sugar until thick peaks form; fold in chestnut mixture. Spoon into large piping bag fitted with star tube, pipe mixture into small serving dishes or glasses. Spread almond flakes on to oven tray, toast in moderate oven 5 minutes or until golden brown; cool. Sprinkle almond flakes over chestnut cream, drizzle with melted chocolate. Refrigerate until ready to serve. Serves 4.

Note: There are two types of canned chestnuts. One is pure chestnuts pureed; the other is pureed chestnuts flavoured with sugar, glucose and vanilla. The latter is the type to use for this recipe.

STRAWBERRY-BRANDY SNAPS

2 tablespoons golden syrup
60g (2oz) butter
⅓ cup brown sugar
¼ cup plain flour
2 teaspoons ground ginger
pinch salt
FILLING
2 cups cream
1 tablespoon sugar
2 tablespoons grand marnier
1 punnet strawberries

Put syrup, butter and brown sugar into saucepan. Stir over low heat until butter has melted. Sift flour, ginger and salt into bowl, stir in butter mixture; mix well. Drop small teaspoonfuls of mixture on to greased trays, allowing room for spreading. Bake in moderate oven approximately 5 minutes or until golden brown. Remove from oven; allow to cool on trays 1 minute before putting on wire racks to cool.

Filling: Wash and hull strawberries, reserve 3 whole strawberries for decoration. Slice remaining strawberries in half. Place cream, sugar and grand marnier into bowl, beat until firm peaks form. Sandwich three brandy snap biscuits together with cream and sliced strawberries. Top each with whipped cream and reserved strawberry half. If desired, reserved strawberries can first be glazed with a little warmed, sieved strawberry jam. Serves 6.

Strawberry-brandy snaps.

Strawberry water ice.

Hot Desserts

Hot desserts are perfect to keep the family happy in winter weather. Here are puddings they'll hurry home to enjoy

BRANDIED CARAMEL APPLES
60g (2oz) butter
½ cup brown sugar, firmly packed
4 large green apples
2 tablespoons brandy
½ teaspoon cinnamon
pinch nutmeg
pinch mixed spice

Peel apples, cut into quarters, remove cores, cut into slices. Melt butter in frying pan, add sugar, stir until combined. Add apples, stir until apples are coated with caramel. Add remaining ingredients, bring to boil, boil 3 minutes. Serve with cream. Serves 4.

BANANA FRITTERS
8 bananas
3 tablespoons plain flour
⅓ cup cornflour
1½ teaspoons baking powder
¼ teaspoon salt
½ cup milk
1 egg white
½ cup castor sugar

Peel bananas, cut in half. Sift flour, cornflour, baking powder and salt into bowl. Mix to smooth batter with the milk. Beat egg white until soft peaks form, fold lightly into batter. Drop banana pieces into batter, then deep-fry in hot oil until golden brown. Remove and drain on absorbent paper. Toss in sugar, serve hot with ice-cream or cream. Serves 4.

RHUBARB AND APPLE CRUMBLE
1 bunch rhubarb (approximately 16 sticks)
2 green apples
¼ cup sugar
2 tablespoons water
CRUMBLE TOPPING
¾ cup cornflakes
¼ cup coconut
¼ cup brown sugar, firmly packed
¼ cup condensed milk

Wash and trim rhubarb, cut into 2.5cm (1in) pieces. Peel and core apples, cut into quarters, slice thinly. Put rhubarb and apple in saucepan with sugar and water. Cook, covered, over medium heat until tender (approximately 10 to 15 minutes). Spoon rhubarb mixture into one large or 4 individual heatproof dishes, sprinkle topping over rhubarb. Bake in moderate oven 10 to 15 minutes or until topping is golden brown. Serve topped with whipped cream or with ice-cream.

Crumble Topping: Combine cornflakes, coconut, brown sugar and condensed milk. Mix well. Serves 4.

HOT APRICOTS WITH SOUR CREAM
470g (15oz) can apricot halves
½ cup sugar
2 tablespoons self-raising flour
1 cup sour cream
1 egg
1 teaspoon vanilla
TOPPING
2 tablespoons sugar
1 teaspoon cinnamon
2 teaspoons butter

Combine sugar and flour, add sour cream, egg and vanilla: beat until smooth. Drain apricots. Put apricots in base of 20cm (8in) pie plate. Spoon over the sour cream mixture. Bake in moderate oven 35 minutes. Remove from oven, sprinkle with topping. Return to oven for 10 minutes.

Topping: Combine sugar and cinnamon. Rub in the butter. Serves 4.

APPLE BREAD AND BUTTER PUDDING
5 apples
¼ cup sugar
2 tablespoons water
6 thin slices bread
butter
2½ cups milk
3 eggs
1 tablespoon sugar, extra
1 tablespoon grated lemon rind
1 cup sultanas
TOPPING
30g (1oz) butter
2 tablespoons coconut
3 tablespoons sugar
½ cup self-raising flour

Peel and core apples, cut into slices. Place apples, sugar and water in saucepan; cook, covered, 5 to 10 minutes until apple is reduced to pulp. Butter bread lightly, remove crusts. Arrange slices in layers in greased ovenproof dish; spread each layer generously with apple pulp and sprinkle with lemon rind and sultanas. Beat together eggs, milk and extra sugar, pour over bread. Let stand 15 minutes, then sprinkle topping over. Bake in moderately slow oven 40 minutes. Serve with cream or custard.

Topping: Sift flour, add coconut and sugar. Rub in butter until mixture resembles breadcrumbs. Serves 4 to 6.

BUTTERSCOTCH APPLE DUMPLINGS
2 green apples
1 cup self-raising flour
pinch salt
2 teaspoons sugar
60g (2oz) butter
2 tablespoons water, approximately
SAUCE
30g (1oz) butter
1 cup brown sugar, lightly packed
1 tablespoon golden syrup
1½ cups water

Sift flour and salt into bowl, add sugar; rub in butter. Add water, mix to a soft dough; a little extra water may be

Banana fritters.

Hot Desserts

needed. Peel, quarter and core apples. Divide pastry into 8 equal portions, carefully press each portion of pastry round an apple quarter. Put in ovenproof dish, pour sauce over. Bake, uncovered, in moderate oven 25 to 30 minutes or until pastry is golden. Serve warm with ice-cream or cream.

Sauce: Combine all ingredients in saucepan, stir over low heat until sugar is dissolved, bring to boil, remove from heat. Serves 4.

CHOCOLATE SOUFFLE
2 eggs, separated
60g (2oz) butter
2 tablespoons plain flour
½ teaspoon salt
½ cup milk
2 tablespoons sugar
125g (4oz) dark chocolate

Melt butter in top of double saucepan over simmering water, remove from heat. Stir in flour and salt, stir until smooth and free of lumps. Stir in milk all at once. Return to heat, stir over simmering water until smooth and thick. Remove from heat. Stir in grated chocolate and sugar while still hot. Stir until dissolved; cool mixture slightly. Beat egg yolks until pale and fluffy, gradually stir into chocolate mixture with thin-edged metal spoon or spatula. Using clean bowl, beat egg whites until short moist peaks form. Using thin-edged metal spoon or spatula, fold half the egg whites into chocolate mixture, then fold in remaining egg whites. Spoon mixture evenly into four greased small individual souffle dishes (approximately ½-cup capacity). Fill mixture to within 1cm (½in) of top. Bake in moderate oven 15 to 20 minutes. Serves 4.

CARAMEL BAKED APPLES
6 green apples
1½ teaspoons cinnamon
1 cup brown sugar, lightly packed
2 tablespoons plain flour
1½ cups water
30g (1oz) butter

Core apples; do not peel. Make a slit around centre of apples so that apples do not burst during cooking. Place apples in ovenproof dish. Sprinkle over combined cinnamon, sugar and flour. Add water to pan and place a piece of butter on top of each apple. Bake uncovered in moderate oven 1 hour or until apples are tender. Stir sauce occasionally during cooking time. Serves 6.

STEAMED DATE PUDDING
500g (1lb) dates
90g (3oz) butter
¾ cup brown sugar, firmly packed
¾ cup water
1 tablespoon vinegar
2 eggs
1 tablespoon rum or sherry
2 cups plain flour
½ cup self-raising flour
1 teaspoon bicarbonate of soda
1 teaspoon cinnamon
½ cup milk

Put chopped dates, butter, brown sugar and water in saucepan, stir over low heat until butter melts and sugar dissolves, increase heat, bring to boil, reduce heat, simmer 5 minutes. Remove from heat, add vinegar, cool. Add combined beaten eggs and rum or sherry, mix well. Fold in sifted dry ingredients alternately with the milk, mix well. Spoon mixture evenly into greased 2-litre (approximately 4-pint) pudding basin, cover, steam 2 to 2½ hours or until cooked. Serve hot with custard. Serves 4 to 6.

APPLE-SULTANA SLICE
PASTRY
2 cups self-raising flour
2 tablespoons custard powder
½ teaspoon cinnamon
90g (3oz) butter

Steamed date pudding.

Apple-sultana slice.

1 teaspoon grated lemon rind
⅓ cup sugar
1 egg yolk
⅓ cup milk, approximately
FILLING
410g (13oz) can pie apple
1 tablespoon lemon juice
1 tablespoon water
1 teaspoon grated lemon rind
¼ cup sultanas
1 tablespoon honey
icing sugar

Pastry: Sift dry ingredients into bowl, rub in butter until mixture resembles fine breadcrumbs; add lemon rind and sugar, mix well. Beat egg yolk and milk together, add to dry ingredients, mix to firm dough. Knead lightly on floured surface. Roll out two-thirds of pastry to line greased 28cm by 18cm (11in by 7in) lamington

tin, bringing pastry half-way up sides of tin. Put cooled apple filling into pastry, trickle honey over apple. Roll out remaining one-third of pastry, cut into 5mm (¼in) wide strips and arrange in lattice fashion over apple; seal edges. Bake in moderately hot oven 10 minutes, reduce heat to moderate, cook further 15 minutes or until pastry is cooked. Dust with icing sugar while still hot. (The hot apple absorbs the icing sugar, leaving a snowy covering on the pastry.)

Filling: Put apple, lemon rind, water, lemon juice and sultanas in pan, stir over low heat for 3 minutes, cool.

APPLE STRUDEL
375g (12oz) pkt puff pastry
3 green apples

½ cup sultanas
¼ cup brown sugar, lightly packed
1 teaspoon grated lemon rind
½ teaspoon cinnamon
1 tablespoon sweet sherry
melted butter

Put thawed pastry on to lightly floured board, roll to oblong shape approximately 25cm by 35cm (10in by 14in). Spread prepared filling to within 2.5cm (1in) of edges. Roll up pastry from the long side, seal edges. Put on lightly greased oven tray, brush with melted butter, bake in moderately hot oven 15 to 20 minutes or until pastry is golden brown. Serve with cream or custard.

Filling: Peel and core apples, slice very thinly, stir in sultanas, brown sugar, lemon rind, cinnamon and sherry. Serves 4.

Jams

When fruit is in season capture its full flavour with home-made jam — sweetly delicious and so easy to make

MARMALADE
4 oranges
2 lemons
1.25 litres (5 cups) water
1.5 kg (3lb) sugar

Wash fruit, cut in half lengthwise. Cut each half into thin slices, using a very sharp knife. Remove seeds. Put fruit into bowl, add water, cover, let stand overnight. Next day put fruit and water into large saucepan. Bring to boil, reduce heat. Cover and simmer 40 minutes. Put sugar into baking dish, place in moderate oven for 7 minutes. Add sugar to fruit mixture, stir until sugar is dissolved. Bring to boil. Boil rapidly, uncovered, for 45 to 55 minutes. After 40 minutes, start testing jam to see if it is set. Spoon small amount on to cold saucer (put saucer in refrigerator when starting to make jam), refrigerate for 2 to 3 minutes. Push a spoon on to jam; if jam crinkles it is set. Remove saucepan from heat while testing jam. Skim any scum from top. Let cool slightly to allow fruit to settle. Pour into sterilized jars; seal. Makes approximately 1.75 litres.

Marmalade.

Jams

STRAWBERRY AND APPLE JAM

500g (1lb) strawberries (approximately 2 punnets)
3 large green apples
¼ cup lemon juice
3 cups water
1 kg (2lb) sugar

Wash and hull strawberries. Peel, quarter and core apples, cut quarters into very thin slices. Put halved strawberries, apples, lemon juice and water into large pan. Bring to boil, reduce heat, simmer covered for 20 minutes or until apples are very tender. Put sugar into baking dish, place in moderate oven for 7 minutes. Add sugar to strawberry mixture, stir until sugar is dissolved. Increase heat, bring mixture to boil, boil steadily uncovered for 25 minutes or until jam jells when tested on cold saucer. Pour into hot sterilized jars; seal. Makes approximately 1.5 litres.

PAPAW AND GINGER JAM

1 medium papaw, approximately 750g (1½lb), not too ripe
90g (3oz) preserved ginger
½ cup lemon juice
2 cups sugar

Peel papaw, remove seeds, chop roughly. Put papaw and chopped ginger into pan, add lemon juice, bring to boil. Boil until fruit is tender, approximately 5 minutes. Reduce heat, add sugar, stir over low heat until sugar is dissolved. Bring to boil. Boil rapidly uncovered for 25 minutes or until jam jells when tested on cold saucer. Stir jam occasionally during cooking time. Pour jam into hot sterilized jars. Makes approximately 625ml (2½ cups).

APRICOT AND PINEAPPLE JAM

500g (1lb) dried apricots
1 small pineapple
1.5 litres (6 cups) water
¼ cup lemon juice
1kg (2lb) sugar

Chop apricots roughly. Put apricots and water into large bowl, allow to stand 2 hours. Put apricot mixture into large saucepan, bring to boil, reduce heat; simmer, covered, for 30 minutes. Add peeled, cored and finely chopped pineapple, cover, simmer a further 15 minutes. Put sugar into large baking dish, place in moderate oven for 7 minutes. Add sugar to apricot mixture, stir until sugar is dissolved. Add lemon juice, bring to boil, reduce heat so that mixture is at a fast simmer; cook for 30 minutes or until jam jells when tested on cold saucer. Stir jam frequently during cooking time. Pour into hot sterilized jars; seal. Makes approximately 2 litres.

WHISKY MARMALADE

6 oranges (about 1kg)
2 lemons (about 500g)
1.5 litres (6 cups water)
2kg (4lb) sugar
¼ cup whisky

Cut fruit into quarters. Cut each quarter into thin slices. Put fruit into large bowl, add water, cover bowl, allow to stand overnight. Next day, put fruit with the water into large pan, bring to boil, reduce heat, simmer covered for 20 minutes or until rind is very tender. Put sugar into baking dish, place in moderate oven for 7 minutes. Add sugar to fruit mixture, stir until dissolved. Bring to boil, boil uncovered for about 30 minutes or until jam jells when tested on cold saucer. Add whisky, stir until combined, remove from heat. Pour into hot sterilized jars; seal. Makes approximately 2 litres.

TOMATO JAM

1.5kg (3lb) tomatoes
500g (1lb) apples (approximately 3 medium apples)
1 tablespoon grated lemon rind
⅓ cup lemon juice
1.25kg (2½lb) sugar

Skin tomatoes and cut into thin slices. Put tomatoes, peeled, cored and thinly sliced apples and grated lemon rind into large saucepan, cover, bring to boil, reduce heat, simmer 30 minutes. Put sugar into baking dish, place in moderate oven for 7 minutes. Add sugar and lemon juice to tomato mixture, stir until sugar is dissolved. Bring to boil. Boil approximately 40 to 45 minutes or until jam jells when tested on cold saucer. Stir jam occasionally during cooking time. Pour into hot sterilized jars; seal. Makes approximately 1.5 litres.

Strawberry and apple jam.

Sweet Butters

These are lovely on hot toast or scones, or as fillings for small cakes and tartlets

LEMON BUTTER
4 eggs
¾ cup sugar
½ cup lemon juice
¼ cup water
2 teaspoons grated lemon rind
125g (4oz) butter

Put beaten eggs and sugar into top of double saucepan, stir until combined. Gradually add lemon juice and water, stir until combined. Add lemon rind and roughly chopped butter. Place pan over simmering water, stir until mixture thickly coats the back of wooden spoon. Pour into hot sterilized jars; seal. Store in refrigerator. Makes approximately 3 cups.

PASSIONFRUIT AND PINEAPPLE BUTTER
470g (15oz) can crushed pineapple
½ cup passionfruit pulp (approximately 6 passionfruit)
4 eggs
½ cup sugar
90g (3oz) butter
½ teaspoon grated lemon rind

Beat eggs in bowl until combined. Put eggs, undrained pineapple, passionfruit pulp, sugar, chopped butter and lemon rind into top of double saucepan, stir over simmering water until mixture is very thick, approximately 10 minutes. Pour into hot sterilized jars; seal. Store in refrigerator. Makes approximately 3½ cups.

GRAPEFRUIT BUTTER
1 tablespoon grated grapefruit rind
1 cup grapefruit juice
1¼ cups castor sugar
½ cup water
125g (4oz) butter

3 eggs
2 teaspoons gelatine
2 tablespoons water, extra

Place rind, grapefruit juice, sugar, water and roughly chopped butter into top of double saucepan, stir over direct heat until mixture comes to boil, reduce heat, simmer uncovered for 3 minutes; remove pan from heat, allow to cool slightly. Place eggs in bowl, beat until frothy, gradually. add grapefruit mixture, stir until combined. Sprinkle gelatine over extra water, stir until combined, stand over hot water until gelatine dissolves. Add gelatine to grapefruit mixture. Place pan over saucepan of simmering water, stir until mixture is thick, approximately 8 minutes. Pour into hot sterilized jars; seal. Store in refrigerator. Makes approximately 3¼ cups.

ORANGE BUTTER
⅔ cup sugar
2 teaspoons grated lemon rind
2 teaspoons grated orange rind
4 egg yolks
1 cup orange juice
¼ cup lemon juice
125g (4oz) butter
1 teaspoon gelatine
2 tablespoons water
30g (1oz) mixed peel

Put sugar, lemon rind, orange rind and egg yolks into top of double saucepan, stir until combined. Gradually add strained orange juice and lemon juice, stir until combined. Add chopped butter. Place pan over simmering water, stir until mixture thickly coats the back of wooden spoon. Sprinkle gelatine over cold water, stir until combined. Add gelatine mixture to orange butter, stir until gelatine is dissolved. Allow to

become cold, then add finely chopped mixed peel. Pour into hot sterilized jars; seal. Store in refrigerator. Makes approximately 2½ cups.

BANANA BUTTER
4 ripe bananas
⅔ cup sugar
3 eggs
90g (3oz) butter
¼ cup lemon juice
1 tablespoon grated lemon rind
½ cup orange juice

Peel bananas, chop roughly, place into electric blender, blend on medium speed until smooth. If you do not have a blender, mash bananas well. Place mashed bananas, sugar, beaten eggs, chopped butter, strained lemon juice, lemon rind and strained orange juice into top of double saucepan, stir until combined. Stand saucepan over simmering water, stir until mixture thickly coats the back of wooden spoon. Pour into hot sterilized jars; seal. Store in refrigerator. Makes approximately 3½ cups.

PEANUT BUTTER
500g (1lb) unsalted roasted peanuts
½ teaspoon salt
⅓ cup oil, approximately

Place half the peanuts into electric blender, blend on medium speed, gradually adding oil; blend until mixture is smooth and thick. Add remainder of peanuts and salt, blend a few seconds more for crunchy peanut butter; blend longer for smooth peanut butter. A little extra oil may be needed, depending on how quickly the peanuts absorb the oil. Makes approximately 2 cups.

Delicious fruit-flavoured butters make attractive gifts from your kitchen.

PASSIONFRUIT PINEAPPLE BUTTER

ORANGE BUTTER

GRAPEFRUIT BUTTER

LEMON BUTTER

Pickles & Chutneys

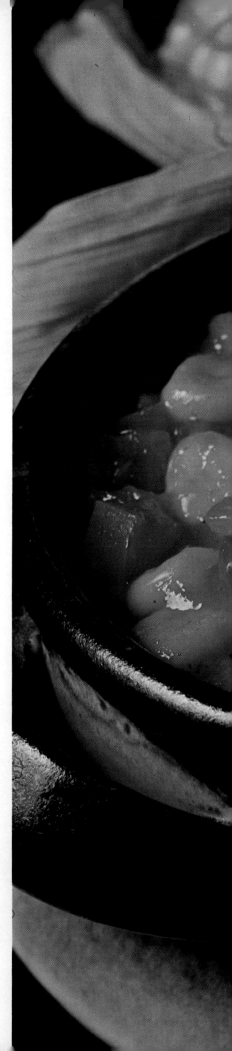

Here's our favourite selection of pickles and chutneys; serve them with hot or cold meats and, of course, they are a special accompaniment for curries

APRICOT CHUTNEY

250g (8oz) dried apricots
2 cups boiling water
185g (6oz) raisins
1½ cups brown sugar, firmly packed
1 cup white vinegar
6 whole cloves
2 teaspoons mustard seeds

Cover apricots with boiling water, stand at least 2 hours. Put apricots and liquid in saucepan with remaining ingredients, stir over low heat until sugar has dissolved, then bring to boil. Reduce heat, simmer uncovered 1 hour or until mixture is thick. Pour into sterilized jars, seal. Makes approximately 1 litre.

CORN RELISH

2 large onions
water
2 cups white vinegar
½ cup sugar
½ teaspoon chilli powder
1 tablespoon curry powder
1 teaspoon turmeric
1 teaspoon mustard seeds
2.5cm (1in) piece green ginger
2 x 470g (15oz) cans corn niblets
1 large carrot
2 sticks celery
1 red pepper
salt, pepper
3 tablespoons cornflour

Peel and chop onions, put into large pan, cover with water. Bring to boil, remove from heat immediately, drain. Put vinegar, sugar, chilli powder, curry powder, turmeric, mustard seeds and peeled and finely chopped ginger into large pan. Bring to boil, reduce heat, simmer uncovered 2 minutes. Add drained corn (reserve liquid), onions, peeled and diced carrot, chopped celery, seeded and chopped red pepper. Bring to boil, reduce heat, simmer 10 minutes. Combine cornflour with reserved corn liquid, gradually add to corn mixture, stir until boiling. Reduce heat, simmer uncovered 5 minutes, stirring occasionally. Season with salt and pepper. Pour into hot sterilized jars. Makes approximately 2 litres.

Corn relish.

Pickles & Chutneys

PICKLED ONIONS

2kg (4lb) small onions
750g (1½lb) salt
water
1.25 litres (5 cups) white vinegar
4 teaspoons salt, extra
2 teaspoons ground ginger
1½ teaspoons whole allspice
1½ teaspoons whole cloves
2.5cm (1in) cinnamon stick
6 whole peppercorns

Place unpeeled onions and 750g salt in large bowl, add enough water to cover, stand 2 days, stirring occasionally. Drain liquid, peel onions. Cover onions with boiling water, stand 3 minutes, drain. Repeat this boiling water and draining process twice more. Pack onions into hot sterilized jars. Combine all remaining ingredients in a saucepan, bring slowly to boil, reduce heat, simmer 10 minutes. Cool slightly, strain, pour over onions, seal.

TOMATO RELISH

1.5kg (3lb) ripe tomatoes
500g (1lb) onions
2 tablespoons salt
2 cups sugar
3 teaspoons curry powder
¼ teaspoon chilli powder
1 tablespoon dry mustard
2 cups brown vinegar

Skin tomatoes, cut into cubes, place in bowl. Peel onions, chop finely, place in separate bowl. Sprinkle each with 1 tablespoon salt, cover, leave overnight. Next day place tomatoes and their liquid and onions together in saucepan. Add sugar, stir over low heat until dissolved, increase heat, bring to boil, boil covered 5 minutes. Combine curry powder, chilli powder and mustard, mix to a smooth paste with a little of the vinegar, add remaining vinegar, add to saucepan, stir to combine thoroughly. Bring to boil, boil uncovered 50 to 60 minutes or until thick. Pour relish into sterilized jars, cool and seal. Makes approximately 1 litre.

CURRIED CUCUMBER PICKLES

6 medium cucumbers
3 onions
3 green or red peppers
½ cup salt
water
3¼ cups white vinegar
2 cups sugar
2 teaspoons curry powder
1 teaspoon celery seeds
1 teaspoon mustard seeds

Wash cucumbers, cut into 5mm (¼in) slices. Peel and slice onions, cut peppers into 1cm (½in) pieces. Put vegetables in earthenware or plastic bowl, sprinkle with the salt, pour water over to cover vegetables, stand 5 hours, drain well. Combine vinegar, sugar, curry powder, celery seeds and mustard seeds in saucepan. Stir over low heat until sugar is dissolved, bring to boil. Add drained vegetables, bring back to boil, pour into sterilized jars, seal. Makes approximately 2.5 litres.

GREEN TOMATO PICKLES

2kg (4lb) green tomatoes
1kg (2lb) onions
½ small cauliflower
1 small cucumber
2 litres (8 cups) water
¼ cup salt
½ cup flour
2½ cups brown sugar, firmly packed
1½ teaspoons dry mustard
2 teaspoons turmeric
¼ teaspoon cayenne
½ teaspoon curry powder
2½ cups brown vinegar

Chop tomatoes, peel and chop onions, chop cauliflower into flowerets, peel and chop cucumber. Put all vegetables in large bowl, pour over water, add salt; cover, allow to stand overnight. Next day put vegetables and liquid in large saucepan, bring to boil, boil 2 minutes, drain. In another saucepan combine flour, brown sugar, mustard, turmeric, cayenne and curry powder, mix to a smooth paste with a little of the vinegar, add remaining vinegar. Stir over heat until mixture boils and thickens. Add drained vegetables, bring back to the boil, boil 1 minute. Remove from heat, bottle and seal. Makes approximately 2 litres.

Green tomato pickles and, at right, Tomato relish.

Confectionery

These recipes will produce fast sellers at fetes; or make them for sweet eating at any time

CARAMELS
1 cup castor sugar
90g (3oz) butter
2 tablespoons golden syrup
⅓ cup liquid glucose
½ cup condensed milk
1 teaspoon vanilla

Combine all ingredients except vanilla in saucepan, stir over low heat until sugar has dissolved, increase heat, boil 10 minutes, stirring constantly. Mixture will be dark caramel colour. Add vanilla, pour immediately into well greased 20cm (8in) slab tin. Mark into squares while hot, allow to cool, then break into squares.

COCONUT ICE
4 cups sugar
1 cup milk
2 tablespoons liquid glucose
250g (8oz) coconut
pink food colouring

Place sugar, milk and glucose into saucepan, stir over low heat until sugar has dissolved. Brush down sides of saucepan with hot water, making sure there are no crystals on sides of pan. Bring to boil steadily to 112C (235F) or until a small amount, when dropped into cold water, forms soft ball when rolled between the fingers. Remove from heat, divide mixture between 2 bowls, allow to cool slightly, add half coconut to each bowl. Stir first mixture until thick and creamy, press into greased and greased paper lined 20cm (8in) slab tin. Colour remaining mixture pink with food colouring, beat until thick and creamy, press on to white mixture. When cold, remove coconut ice from tin, cut into squares.

TOASTED MARSHMALLOWS
4 tablespoons gelatine
1 cup cold water
4 cups sugar
2 cups boiling water
2 teaspoons vanilla
2 teaspoons lemon juice
250g (8oz) coconut

Sprinkle gelatine over cold water. Put sugar and boiling water into large saucepan, stir over low heat until sugar is dissolved, bring to boil. Stir in gelatine mixture. Boil steadily, uncovered, 20 minutes. Allow to cool to lukewarm. Pour mixture into large bowl of electric mixer, add vanilla and lemon juice. Beat on high speed until very thick and white. Pour into two deep 20cm (8in) square cake tins which have been rinsed out with cold water. Refrigerate until set. Put coconut in heavy pan. Stir with wooden spoon over moderate heat until coconut is light golden brown. Remove from pan immediately or coconut will continue to cook in heat of pan. Cut marshmallow into squares with wet knife while still in the tin. Lift out with small spatula, toss in toasted coconut. Keep refrigerated.

TOFFEES
3 cups sugar
1 cup water
¼ cup brown malt vinegar

Place sugar, water and vinegar into saucepan, stir over low heat until sugar is dissolved. Increase heat, boil rapidly uncovered for approximately 15 minutes or until a small amount, when poured into cold water, will crack. Remove from heat, stand saucepan in cold water for 1 minute. Remove from water, allow bubbles to subside. Pour into paper patty cases. Leave 2 minutes before decorating with coconut, hundreds and thousands, etc. Makes 12.

BUTTERSCOTCH
2 cups sugar
⅓ cup water
⅔ cup liquid glucose
125g (4oz) butter
1 teaspoon lemon essence
½ teaspoon salt

Combine sugar, water and glucose in heavy saucepan, stir over low heat until sugar is dissolved. Bring to boil, reduce heat until very low (mixture will still boil), boil 8 to 10 minutes or to 150C (300F) on sweets thermometer; mixture should be light golden brown. Remove from heat, add remaining ingredients, stir until well blended. Pour into lightly greased 18cm by 28cm (7in by 11in) lamington tin. Mark into squares while still hot.

Coconut ice.

120

Christmas Cookery

Christmas cookery is probably the most important of the year. Here are our best recipes for all the wonderful foods of Christmas

CHRISTMAS PUDDING
1kg (2lb) mixed fruit
250g (8oz) dates
250g (8oz) raisins
2 cups water
1 cup white sugar
1 cup brown sugar, lightly packed
1 teaspoon salt
250g (8oz) butter
2 teaspoons bicarbonate of soda
3 eggs
2 cups plain flour
2 cups self-raising flour
2 teaspoons mixed spice
1 teaspoon cinnamon
¼ cup rum

Place in pan the fruit, roughly chopped dates, raisins, water, sugars, salt and butter. Stir over low heat until butter has melted, simmer mixture 8 minutes, stirring occasionally; remove from heat, stir in soda. Allow to stand until mixture is completely cold. Lightly beat together eggs and rum, stir into cold mixture. Add sifted flours, mixed spice and cinnamon, mix well.

To steam: Fill into well-greased 4 litre (approximately 8 pint) pudding basin. Steam 6 hours; replenish with boiling water every 20 minutes. Re-steam 2 hours on day of serving.

To boil: Follow the step-by-step instructions on page 124. Boil rapidly 6 hours, replenish with boiling water every 20 minutes; water must not go off boil. Reboil 2 hours on day of serving.

FAMILY-SIZE PUDDING
250g (8oz) butter
1 cup brown sugar, firmly packed
1 tablespoon grated orange rind
1 tablespoon grated lemon rind
4 eggs
250g (8oz) dates
250g (8oz) raisins
250g (8oz) sultanas
1 small apple
1 small carrot
125g (4oz) mixed peel
2 cups fresh breadcrumbs
1½ cups plain flour
pinch salt
½ teaspoon nutmeg
1 teaspoon mixed spice
½ teaspoon bicarbonate of soda
3 tablespoons brandy

Cream butter and sugar until light and fluffy. Add orange and lemon rinds. Add eggs one at a time, beating well after each addition. Chop dates, raisins and peel; peel and grate apple and carrot. Stir fruit, carrot, peel and breadcrumbs into creamed mixture. Sift dry ingredients, fold in; add brandy.

To steam: Fill into well-greased 2.5 litre (approximately 4½ pint) pudding basin, steam for 4 hours. Re-steam 2 hours on day of serving.

To boil: Follow the step-by-step instructions on page 124. Boil rapidly 4 hours, replenish with boiling water every 20 minutes; water must not go off boil. Reboil 2 hours on day of serving.

Christmas pudding.

Boiled Christmas Pudding

THERE'S no more popular pudding at Christmas than the boiled pudding — rich, moist and spicily fragrant. Whichever recipe you use, this is how to cook the pudding so that it will turn out perfectly on Christmas Day.

Step 1: Chop fruit so that all pieces are of even size, about the size of a sultana; scissors are best for this. Dip them in water occasionally if fruit is sticky. When fruit is ready, make up pudding mixture as recipe directs, then prepare the pudding cloth.

Step 2: Use a 62cm (25in) square of unbleached calico. Drop it into a large pan of boiling water, boil 30 minutes. Remove from water, wring out well (protect hands from hot cloth with rubber gloves). Spread out cloth and cover liberally with plain flour; about half a cup. The cloth can be left unfloured but flouring gives pudding a better skin. Put pudding mixture into centre of cloth; it should be round in shape, mounded into a slight peak at top. Gather corners and sides of cloth round pudding mixture as evenly as possible. Pull corners tightly and firmly to give pudding a good round shape.

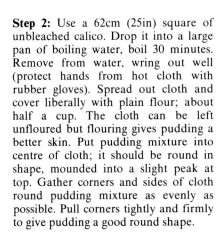

Step 3: Tie firmly with string about 2.5cm (1in) above top of pudding mixture; this allows room for expansion during cooking. Twist string round cloth about 10 times to give good, firm seal. Make handle from string ends to lift out pudding easily when cooked.

Step 4: Have ready a large boiler three-quarters full of boiling water; there must be enough rapidly boiling water to float pudding. Lower pudding into water, put on lid immediately, boil rapidly for time specified in recipe. Replenish with more boiling water about every 20 minutes as water evaporates; water must never go off boil.

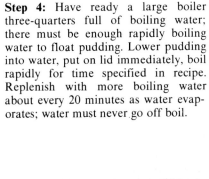

Step 5: At end of cooking time, lift pudding from water, suspend from handle of cupboard door or legs of an upturned stool; pudding must be able to swing freely, without touching anything. Tie ends of wet cloth together so that they do not touch pudding. Leave hang overnight. In hot Christmas weather it is better to store pudding in refrigerator until needed. On day of serving, reboil for time specified in recipe.

SAUCES FOR THE PUDDING

Here is a choice of two sauces to serve with Christmas pudding — one a rich, creamy custard, the other the popular Brandy Butter or Hard Sauce.

BRANDY CUSTARD

¼ cup sugar
½ cup water
2 egg yolks
pinch salt
2 tablespoons brandy
¼ cup cream

Place sugar and water in saucepan, stir over low heat until sugar dissolves. Bring to the boil, reduce heat, simmer 10 minutes. Beat egg yolks and salt, pour in hot syrup slowly, beating until thick and creamy. Fold in brandy and whipped cream.

BRANDY BUTTER (HARD SAUCE)

125g (4oz) butter
2 cups icing sugar
1 tablespoon brandy

Cream butter, gradually blend in sifted icing sugar and brandy. Refrigerate until firm. If desired, when firm, the butter can be put into piping bag fitted with fluted tube and decorative rosettes piped on to a scone tray. Refrigerate again. Grand marnier or cointreau can be used as a delicious alternative to the brandy in this recipe.

RICH FRUIT CAKE

250g (8oz) sultanas
500g (1lb) currants
250g (8oz) raisins
125g (4oz) glace cherries
60g (2oz) mixed peel
1 tablespoon grated orange rind
1 tablespoon grated lemon rind
2 tablespoons lemon juice
½ cup brandy
500g (1lb) butter
1½ cups sugar
4 cups plain flour
1 cup self-raising flour
pinch salt
8 eggs

Place sultanas, currants, roughly chopped raisins, halved cherries, chopped mixed peel, orange rind, lemon rind, lemon juice and brandy in large bowl, mix well. Cover, leave overnight. Cream butter and sugar until light and fluffy, add eggs one at a time, beating well after each addition. Stir in fruit mixture, mix well; add sifted flours and salt. Mix until well combined. Place mixture in deep 25cm (10in) cake tin which has been lined with two thicknesses of brown paper and one thickness of greaseproof paper. Bake in slow oven for approximately 3¼ hours or until cake is cooked when tested with skewer.

IRISH FRUIT CAKE

375g (12oz) sultanas
375g (12oz) raisins
90g (3oz) glace cherries
90g (3oz) dates
60g (2oz) prunes
30g (1oz) glace pineapple
60g (2oz) mixed peel
1 teaspoon grated lemon rind
1 teaspoon grated orange rind
2 tablespoons lemon juice
¼ cup orange juice
⅓ cup whisky
½ small green apple
30g (1oz) walnuts
60g (2oz) ground almonds
185g (6oz) butter
¾ cup castor sugar
3 eggs
1½ cups plain flour
¼ teaspoon nutmeg
½ teaspoon cinnamon
¼ teaspoon salt
1 tablespoon whisky, extra

Stone prunes, chop all fruit, combine in large screwtop jar with rinds, juices, whisky and peeled and grated apple; cover with plastic lid. Shake jar well to mix ingredients evenly; store in cool, dry place 3 weeks. (This gives rich flavour to the fruit). Reverse jar each day. Line deep 20cm (8in) square cake tin with two thicknesses of greaseproof paper, bringing paper 5cm (2in) above edges of tin. Chop walnuts. Beat butter until soft, add sugar, beat only until combined. Add eggs one at a time, beating well after each addition. Put fruit mixture into large basin, add walnuts, almonds and creamed mixture; mix well. Stir in sifted dry ingredients. Spread mixture evenly into prepared tin, bake in slow oven 3 to 3½ hours. Remove from oven, brush evenly with extra whisky, cover with aluminium foil, leave until cold. Remove from tin, re-wrap in foil until required.

FRUIT MINCE PIE

185g (6oz) butter
½ cup castor sugar
2 eggs
3 cups plain flour
⅓ cup ground rice
½ teaspoon baking powder
1 egg white, extra

Cream butter and sugar, add eggs one at a time, beating well after each addition. Sift flour, ground rice and baking powder, work into creamed mixture, knead lightly until smooth. Refrigerate 45 minutes. Roll out half the pastry, line greased 23cm (9in) pie plate, fill with fruit mince (see below). Brush edge with egg white. Roll out remaining pastry, place in position over pie, decorate edges. Brush top of pie with lightly beaten egg white. Bake in moderately hot oven 10 minutes, reduce heat to moderate, bake further 30 minutes.

FRUIT MINCE

470g (15oz) can crushed pineapple
1 cup sultanas
1 cup raisins
¼ cup currants
60g (2oz) glace cherries
1 tablespoon chopped mixed peel
1 apple
¼ cup brown sugar
1 tablespoon grated lemon rind
½ teaspoon cinnamon
½ teaspoon nutmeg
1 tablespoon cornflour
¼ cup brandy

Peel and grate apple. Combine all ingredients — except cornflour and brandy — in saucepan. Stir over medium heat until mixture boils, reduce heat, simmer 3 minutes or until fruit is plump. Blend cornflour with brandy, mix into hot fruit mixture. Stir until mixture boils and thickens. Cool before spreading into pie shell.

Index

Cup and Spoon Measurements

All spoon measurements are level.

To ensure accuracy in your recipes use the standard metric measuring equipment approved by Standards Australia:

(a) 250 millilitre cup for measuring liquids. A litre jug (capacity 4 cups) is also available.

(b) a graduated set of four cups – measuring 1 cup, half, third and quarter cup – for items such as flour, sugar, etc. When measuring in these fractional cups, level off at the brim.

(c) a graduated set of four spoons: tablespoon (20 millilitre liquid capacity), teaspoon (5 millilitre), half and quarter teaspoons. The Australian, British and American teaspoon each has 5ml capacity.

Approximate cup and spoon conversion chart

Australian	American & British
1 cup	1¼ cups
¾ cup	1 cup
⅔ cup	¾ cup
½ cup	⅔ cup
⅓ cup	½ cup
¼ cup	⅓ cup
2 tablespoons	¼ cup
1 tablespoon	3 teaspoons

Note: NZ, USA and UK all use 15ml tablespoons.

We have used large eggs with an average weight of 61g each in all recipes

Oven Temperatures

Electric	C°	F°
Very slow	120	250
Slow	150	300
Moderately slow	160-180	325-350
Moderate	180-200	375-400
Moderately hot	210-230	425-450
Hot	240-250	475-500
Very hot	260	525-550

Gas		
Very slow	120	250
Slow	150	300
Moderately slow	160	325
Moderate	180	350
Moderately hot	190	375
Hot	200	400
Very hot	230	450